CANADA
MASSAGES THE
WORLD

DONALD W.C. HARRIS

authorHOUSE®

AuthorHouse™
1663 Liberty Drive
Bloomington, IN 47403
www.authorhouse.com
Phone: 1 (800) 839-8640

Published by AuthorHouse 09/13/2017

ISBN: 978-1-5462-0476-3 (sc)
ISBN: 978-1-5462-0474-9 (hc)
ISBN: 978-1-5462-0475-6 (e)

Library of Congress Control Number: 2017912723

Print information available on the last page.

ACKNOWLEDGEMENTS

I thank Bukola Okedara for her enthusiasm and energy in initiating and facilitating this book's publication and Dr. Arthur Clark, for introducing Bukola to me, as well as for his efforts to make Calgary a good example of ONENESS cooperation and harmonious interactions of people from diverse cultures.

My gratitude also goes to dear wife Marlene Harris, who provided much help with typing, and to son Jonathan Harris, who willingly gave essential computer assistance.

Much appreciation is due the many reverends, mediums, healers and speakers at Calgary First Spiritualist Church, Canada, along with the tutors from Arthur Findlay College, UK, for their invaluable encouragement, inspiration and guidance.

CONTENTS

LOVE

NATURE

ONENESS/LEADERSHIP

PEACE

TIME

PREFACE

They all came through spirit and I had to do it!

BIOGRAPHY

Donald W.C. Harris, a retired professional geoscientist, spent nearly three decades researching, finding, and developing Canada's mineral and petroleum resources. He demonstrated strong team dedication as well as independent leadership skills in these undertakings.

Don graduated at U of T from Honours Geological Sciences (1960) and continued doctoral research at Alberta universities focusing on biostratigraphy and palaeontology. Garnering academic awards, he taught many undergraduate students in Alberta.

Don miraculously survived a childhood accident resulting in skull fracture, after which he knew he must have been saved for some good reason. Seventy years later, having received hundreds of Spirit-driven inspirational messages that he quickly wrote down as rhyming poems during the last dozen years, Don knows his new purpose is to alert the collective world conscience to the awareness of Oneness and to spread love and respect globally for the sake of Humanity and Nature.

DEDICATION

This book is dedicated to the Spirit team that provided life-changing wisdom through messages intended for my growth, and obviously, for the well-being of all that is, as the world begins to recognize the need to change course by adopting the virtuous principles of ONENESS.

CELEBRATIONS

ALL ABOUT EVERYTHING

Long ago...some forty-three years,
You and I met and conquered some fears...
Enough to stay wed for all of those years,
Even though sometimes, we had shed some tears.

I thought that I knew just where I was heading.
Before I met you, I knew my tough sledding
Would steer me straight on the path I was treading;
My knowledge was solid...my confidence spreading.

Yes it was true...I was all about me.
I'd come way out west to see what I'd see,
To learn rocks and fossils...some geology...
And master the art of a real PhD.

But that never happened to let me be free
To research and teach in university.
While there early on, though, luck brought you me;
You opened my eyes and helped me to see...

Life's not about me, and not even just you;
It's all about everyone, even the zoo!
It's not about two or even a few;
Life's all about *everything!* Now that's something new!

Life's not about us; let's not fool ourselves!
Each of us knows if each of us delves
Into the realms of the Universe' shelves,
All affects all! Yes, everything welds!

HAPPY 43ᴿᴰ ANNIVERSARY, MARLENE!

Composed December 18th, 2007, by Donald W. C. Harris, to help put everything in perspective, especially the concept of togetherness.

ANNIVERSARIES

Anniversaries...they come every year,
For many occasions, and sometimes with tear,
But best of all, they bring **loved ones** near,
For a chance to pronounce, "I **love you** my **dear**!"

"And I **love you** too, my **precious one**!"...
Says the partner, "**Our good times** are not yet done...
Together, **we**'ve had moments of wonderful **fun**;
I feel our beginnings have just now begun!

Each **anniversary** brings everything back...
Including the times when we sent out some flak...
Though balanced with **kindness** and cutting some slack,
Somehow, **together**, **we both** found the knack

To keep **our** show running on track day by day,
Knowing **our love** could not **keep us** away
From **each other** for long...**we**'re **both** truly **okay**...
One cares for the **other**, and **together we**'ll stay!

And **together we**'ll **pray**! When the going gets tough...
Nothing will break us...nothing's enough...
To slash **our love bonds**, all made of **right stuff**!
To set **ONE**'s example, no **ONENESS we**'ll slough!

Respectful action in **fairness**, we've found,
Sets all wheels in motion for **symphonic sound**,
Harmonious vibrations spread through the **world**'s ground!
With **ONENESS** of **SPIRIT**...**ALL** is **HEAVENLY** bound!"

MANY HAPPY
ANNIVERSARIES TO ALL!

Written by Donald W. C. Harris, October 24th, 2009.

Best human behavior will prevail.

AT SEVENTY-FOUR

Well, here I am at seventy-four…
Again, I've made it out the door,
Off to play my game once more;
Just realized my joints aren't sore!

Grateful for good health I own,
I do not have one sore bone!
Good deeds done, good seeds sown,
Many dollars to the wind have blown!

Oh well, at least I've kept my sanity,
And done right things for humanity;
That's important for a man like me…
As those older than seventy-three can see!

I got a call from dear brother Ken,
(To pass happy birthday wishes), then
E-mails from friends and gifts to my den;
It's always nice to be remembered, again!

Today, I'll do some favourite things:
Eat out, watch sports, swim in hot springs,
Walk nature's trails, hear songs a bird sings,
Or just watch a butterfly open its wings!

My sun still shines warmly, now,
And cloudless sky makes me glad somehow,
That I'm still here, along with Thou;
Thank you **GOD**; I feel so blessed! Wow!

BODIES AGE!
SPIRITS STAGE…FOREVER!

The above poem was written by Donald W.C. Harris 2010-05-12,
In celebration of the author's reaching his seventy-fourth birthday.

BECOMING SIXTY

Becoming sixty, you think you're old...
But there is proof that theory is cold.
In fact, instead of growing mould,
You are about to discover gold!

On turning sixty years, you see...
Your counting proceeds backwardly,
Until, again, you're twenty-three
And feeling young and fancy free!

So get a smile upon your face,
And be a happy soul, in case
You're needed for a huge embrace,
By everyone in the human race!

Can you imagine how life will be,
Knowing you'll never feel elderly,
But always young at heart, like me...
Only positive and full of chi?

LIFE IS LIKE GOOD WINE; IT IMPROVES WITH AGE!

The above poem was written by Donald W.
C. Harris September 24th, 2008,
for Ken's birthday.

CHRISTMAS TIME, 2009

It's **Christmas** time, two thousand and nine;
We hope **friends** and **families** are feeling fine;
All gathered **together** for dinners, they'll dine.
Everyone's **grateful**! That's a **good** sign!

Outside it's cold with snow on the ground;
Inside by **fires**, there's **warmth** to be found,
With **singing** and **joys** in all **Christmas** sound.
Happy are those **in loving arms** wound!

Folks of all ages, from young to the old,
Are **all included**…none out of the **fold**!
There's **jubilation**; some **stories** are told,
But **valued** the **most** are all **arms that hold**!

ALL need to know that someone does **care**…
And **loves them** just because they are there,
Being themselves! All love is to **share**!
In each of us there's much **love to spare**!

Why do we celebrate **Christmas** on earth?
Remember it clearly for **Jesus' birth**!
GOD sent his **son** to give us **joy** and **mirth**,
ONENESS' FORGIVENESS and **LOVE** without dearth!

ONENESS IS WHOLENESS!
FORGIVE AND GIVE LOVE!

Written by Donald W. C. Harris, December 19ᵗʰ, 2009,
for **ALL** to enjoy and remember.

HAPPY FATHERS' DAY TO US

Happy Fathers' Day to us!
All dads, it's not a day to cuss.
Today, we're free to just discuss,
And know that we've not missed our bus.

We know the plus of being dad;
As parents, we are truly glad.
The best of life we surely had;
We found the power in one gonad!

The best news though, is we're not done;
Our life anew has just begun;
We all could have another son!
New Age Miracles! Dads, we've won!

Fatherhood is one great honour,
Even though she'll think we conned her,
We know without her we're a gonner;
If not for her...we'd all be loners.

BLESS ALL YOU MOTHERS!

Written in honour of all fathers, June 17th,
2007, by Donald W. C. Harris.

DADS BE PROUD!

NEW YEAR'S EVE

New Year's Eve is here once again;
Take some time to just say, "Amen!"...
To love all children, all women, all men,
No matter their hue, their creed or their den.

Each of us needs to stop thinking small,
To listen more closely to hear others call.
No need to be greedy...enough is for all;
Stop being selfish! Play more than fair ball!

Fear in the home means no home at all.

We all can do better, so let's begin now.
There's more to right living than watching the Dow!
Your God, your Allah, Confucius or Tao...
Whoever your "power", let them guide you how.

But trust in yourself to do what you know's right,
Then set out and do it with all of your might.
You'll push all the evils way out of sight...
Make room for Hope sunshine, so warm its white light.

Share to be fair! Care to be kind!
Ensure that no one is left far behind.
Bend over backwards to make ties that bind;
You'll help build a world with feelings refined.

HAPPY NEW YEAR, EVERYONE!

Written for all, December 31st, 2006, by
Donald W. C. Harris, with genuine
hope for a glorious and wonderful world of
universal joy and happiness, soon.

ONE IS NOT SMALL

Becoming **ONE** means everything...
More than being queen or king!
When you are **ONE**, you feel like spring
Every moment; you want to sing!

Being **ONE** means more than all;
And number **ONE** is not small;
It's really biggest of them all!
ONE includes the short and tall,

Plus all the others, on Earth ball!
Every thing can feel the call
Of **ONENESS'** voice, a **SOURCE**-full drawl.
The writing's on the wall, in **ONENESS'** scrawl!

ALL knowing **ONENESS**...that's what's needed,
For **PEACE** and **LOVE!** A world richly seeded
With **SPIRITUAL inspiration** heeded
Yields bountiful crops in gardens...if weeded!

ONENESS means: I **love** you and you **love** me,
Together, **we all love all** and all is **love**ly!
GOD loves all...that's every be-
Ing, bug, bird, flower, grass and tree,

And all the **water** running free,
That fills the **ONE** huge **OCEAN (SEA)**,
And keeps **alive** all **life** there be!
Loving is **key** to **ONE's eternity!**

MAKE ONE OUR BIGGEST
WHOLE NUMBER!

HAPPY BIRTHDAY, RILEY!

The above poem was written by Donald W.C. Harris, 2010-03-31
It was written with love for a grandchild's first birthday celebration.

OUR DUO GUEST

Our welcome west is for the very best…
It's special for you, our duo guest,
We love you both from toe to chest,
Even your heads have passed the test!

Two weeks out here should be such fun;
Both get ready for perfect sun.
Your time is short so you'd better run
To do all things and get them done!

We bet you've brought your golf clubs too,
To play green courses; there are quite a few.
Raft some rivers or just canoe,
And hike some mountains to get the view!

You might have to wet your skin,
With bug spray to keep mosquitoes thin,
To stop their sucking blood within,
But most to help you smile and grin!

Take a walk down to the lake;
Visit friends and grill some steak.
Catch some fish for a breakfast bake;
Enjoy a swim; eat some healthy cake!

Take some pictures before heading back;
While on the plane, enjoy a snack!
Remember: you have filled your pack,
With happy memories 'til you come back!

VACATIONS WORTHY OF CELEBRATIONS!

The above poem was written by Donald W.C. Harris 2010-08-06.
It was written in honour of a special visit by two special people.

THANKSGIVING IS FOR GIVING
THANKS AND FORGIVING

Thanksgiving is for **giving thanks**...
Not for playing nasty pranks,
Not for building warfare tanks,
Not for walking pirates' planks!

Thanksgiving is for **giving forgiving**...
Forgiving yourself...mostly for living
A **life**, thus far, of not forgiving.
I sense you're very cold and shivering!

Warm your **heart** with **kinder thoughts**;
This can end those icy onslaughts...
Soon, you won't feel tied up in knots!
Now, you're sweet, like rind of kumquats.

Now you have entered your new mellow state,
You've chosen to start just feeling great,
For your **heart** has become a **welcoming gate**,
For **accepting ALL others** in their dire strait!

Now as you have **forgiven them ALL**...
All those you blamed for your downfall,
When, in truth, you alone dropped the ball,
And it was just you who missed the call...

You can freely move straight ahead,
Now you, as one grateful leader instead,
Know that you have made your own bed,
With **CLUB ONENESS**! Enough said.

CHOOSE TO FORGIVE...
PEACE WILL FIND YOU!

Written for **ALL** to be **grateful** for the **gift** of **THANKSGIVING**,
by Donald W. C. Harris, October 11th, 2009.

VERY FIRST TIME

For forty-six years we've stuck like glue
Because we've both loved each other true.
We've both endured a sting or two
That irked the devil out of me and you!

When I met you the very first time
At Phil's where you hosted in your prime,
We went for pizza at Tom's House fine,
You drove us to fish at Sibbald Flats sublime!

You were proud of your '37 Plymouth car;
You'd already driven it many miles far!
I felt honoured as your new passenger star:
You were my queen; I felt like your czar!

You really caught me on that fishing trip.
Hook, line and sinker…I thought you were hip!
I wasn't going to let you give me the slip;
Ever since then, you've been sailing my ship!

Well, I have to confess after forty-six years,
And four sons later and grandkids and cheers,
I'm glad we've survived all trials and tears,
So that now we know love instead of fears!

Sex didn't matter after all;
After birth of our boys, we lost that ball!
But we filled our roles as parents tall.
Kids need good parents! If parents fail, kids fall!

HAPPY 46TH ANNIVERSARY, MARLENE! I DO LOVE YOU!

The above poem was written by Donald W.C. Harris 2010-12-12

WHAT YOUR AGE?

Helen, I know not what your age;
I know, though, that we're all on stage;
And to play our role, we must engage
Each with other; ply kind and loving sage!

In playing our parts really well,
If we've done deeds that ring a bell,
And not a single soul can tell,
We'll feel good! Our chests will swell!

All of us should joke and jest,
But also, we need to do our best
In all we undertake to test
Right living skills with zeal and zest.

Your birthday comes year on year;
I hope each time it brings good cheer.
I pray...sense comfort drawing near;
Your peace inside is crystal clear!

If you can shed all ill will,
You'll move forward free of bill,
Being free to create your still,
For just pure value...garbage nil!

I know that you're intelligent;
That you have so much good intent.
So stay on track! Here-in's the scent!
Bless you with my *word-cement*!

HAPPY BIRTHDAY, HELEN!

Written for Helen Burke's birthday, January, 2008, by
Donald W. C. Harris, a friend.

CHILDREN

ADOPTIVE PARENTS...
SPECIAL AND ONE!

Deprived of contact in tender years...
Lack of touch, brought on some tears;
No loving arms subdued your fears...
Child, these needs slowed down your gears!

Now at last, at ten years young,
Dear child, for you, new life's begun...
Your chance to glow in warmth of sun.
Adoptive parents...you're special and **ONE**!

Thanks are due these "parents" that love her;
Praise be given to her nurturing mother,
And to her caring, fostering father.
GOD bless them both to even bother!

Now, dear child, in new home of love;
Your angels guard and guide from above.
So slide yourself into **ONENESS**' glove,
For you belong to **GOD**'s peace dove!

Right things, done right, free the soul,
To see big picture...not the mole;
To climb to peak of any knoll...
Be more to **ALL** of **ONENESS**' goal!

ONENESS NEEDS EVERYONE!
BLESS CHILDREN, FOR THEY
WILL RIGHT THE WORLD!

This poem, written in March, 2009 by Donald W.C. Harris;
was inspired by one of Oprah Winfrey's shows and is dedicated
to children suffering from neglect, abuse, starvation, etc.
I dedicate the above poem to all children who
have suffered from neglect and/or
abuse and/or deprivation-starvation during
formative childhood years.

MOMS AND DADS

With deadbeat **dads** and drunken **moms,**
And many other parental bums,
It's hard to rejuvenate the slums,
Or give much **hope** with meagre crumbs!

With bad examples misguiding their way,
GOD's **blessed children** go oft astray!
Trouble finds them; some fall prey
To evil's influence every day!

All kids are **innocent** when they are **born**!
Behaviour corrupts, as **life paths** get worn!
Minds and bodies get scarred and torn;
Some get lured and entrapped by porn!

What is happening to **OUR families**?
Do not the **parents** hold proper **keys?**
Parents! Take charge of **responsibilities!**
Parents are **potent,** like **bees** and **trees!**

Family strength builds by **love** and **trust;**
Complete **love** and **honesty** are simply a must.
Worthy principles save **ONE**'s pipes from rust!
ONENESS FAMILIES...sprinkles of **SPIRIT**'s cosmic dust!

GREAT PARENTS DO RIGHT!

The above poem was written by Donald W.C. Harris 2010-06-14.
It was written with great love for in-laws, sons and daughters,
grandchildren and grandparents, loving foster parents and
all who do their best to build righteous families.
I wrote the poem while traveling to the hospital to
visit my new grandson and his parents.

MOTHERS

Mothers can sometimes be someone to fear,
But really, they're treasures we need to hold dear.
Mothers are prizes we like to be near,
So give them hugs to make loving them clear.

Mothers are there when our paths have some bumps,
And there to help us climb out of the dumps.
Mothers care for us when we have the mumps;
They know that all of us swallow some lumps.

Mothers mean well with all that they do;
From conception onward, they care deeply for you.
They want what is best for your whole life through;
Knowing all that, you want to love them back too!

Remember that mothers have been here awhile;
Mother Earth and Mother Nature can both make one smile,
And welcome all children of all rank and file!
Make sure you become ONE in tune, ONE in style!

Without all the mothers, where would we be?
Not here in the now…that's easy to see!
All the mothers deserve respect and dignity;
We owe them our lives and love eternally!

Although MOTHER'S DAY comes just once a year,
We're blessed every day, every day that she's here;
Each new day we enjoy having her near…
So say, "Thank you mom! You're really a dear!"

MOMS (DADS TOO) ARE THE GLUE IN FAMILY STEW!

The above poem was written by
Donald W.C. Harris 2010-05-10 & 12.
It was written to honour all moms on Mother's Day.

ONENESS MATH

Baby grandchild, you're part of all,
Of every **person**, short and tall,
Of every **thing** on this earthy ball,
And of **GOD**'s **Universe**, not small!

Baby grandchild, you're **GOD**'s gold mine;
You're part of **HIM, GOD divine!**
We're all **HIS** by **GOD**'s design!
We are what is, on **GOD**'s grapevine!

All is **right** from the very start,
When all **feel love** from the **heart!**
Only time lures **love** apart!
Load only **goodness** in your cart!

Baby grandchild, as you grow strong,
Be gentle, kind, and do no wrong.
Let **heaven** guide your **spirit song!**
Practise love for all time long!

Always forgive so you can **live**,
With inner **peace** that **GOD** will give!
None escape **HIS** training sieve,
ONENESS MATH, GOD's derivative!

Learn from mistakes along the way;
Making some is quite okay!
Do right things right! Do not sway!
Be wise, intuit, and often **pray!**

A CHILD MUST NOT BE DEFILED!

The above poem was written by Donald W.C. Harris 2010-09-26.
The poem was written for all children but inspiration
came from my own grandchildren.

PARENTAL DECAY

A child needs parents to keep it whole,
To be its guardian from head to soul.
And be its protector in a loving role.
A child without parents pays a heavy toll!

Many children are born each day,
Whose mom and/or dad choose to walk away.
Such irresponsibility is simply not okay!
Little lives lose balance from parental decay.

Each child alive deserves more than this.
Each one is **God**'s gift designed to bring bliss;
And each is worthy of loving hugs with a kiss!
Children are precious treasures not to dismiss!

So parents, before you fornicate,
Be sure you've carefully chosen your mate;
And be prepared to step up to the plate,
For children resulting from your steamy hot date!

You've got to be fair to all children who
Come into this world from the actions of you!
So, if you can't handle a baby or few,
Don't mess around! Think! Don't just do!

Respect your partners; honour them too;
Prepare to be with them forever and be true!
Love in a home needs trust through and through!
To make the world better depends upon you!

PARENTAL DECAY
IS NOT THE RIGHT WAY!

The above poem was written by Donald W.C. Harris 2010-12-07.

WHERE HAVE...PARENTS GONE?

Where have all the **parents** gone?
Your **children** need **you** to belong!
Without **your love, they** have no song,
And become prey to the wrong throng.

What have our **moral ethics** become?
How come neighbourhoods are mostly slum?
And why are streets now homes for scum?
What has happened? Were we that numb?

Education is more than school.
Buildings' **teachers** are just one tool!
So much out there is really cool...
Learn from it all! Don't be a fool!

Learn from teachers...from parents...Do!
And sometimes **peers** have the best clue.
Elders are worth attention too.
Every day, learn a thing or two!

Not one person can learn it all;
And no one lives without a fall.
Mistakes occur...Don't make them all!
Wisely heed another's good call!

Back to **parents**...Where should they be?
Attending **kids**, diligently.
Yes, **mom** and **dad**, now you see...
You are **needed**...tremendously!

BE CLOSE FOR YOUR KIDS!

Written by Donald W. C. Harris, November 3rd, 2009, for **all children**.

WORLD ALL CHILDREN WILL WANT

Will **we** leave a world **all children** will want?
Or, one where most suffer…quite frail and gaunt?
A world of imps, who seek someone to taunt…
With air unfit to enjoy runs or jaunt?

Will all land be barren, without any **green**?
Where not much **lives**, without lots of sunscreen?
And the dry winds blow more sand than we've seen?
So much that **kids choke** and **never feel clean**?

Will **friends** help out, or be nasty and mean?
Will less become more than it's ever been?
Will every place become a latrine?
Choose hell…or paradise! Nothing between!

It will not matter what happens out there,
If all **acts** are **governed** by **innermost care**;
Life will be **perfect** when **everything**'s **fair**,
And **each child** is **loved** and **knows ALL will share**!

From **wholesome thoughts**, our **kind actions** spring free;
Then **nothing can limit humanity**…
From overachieving what needs to be…
The **SPIRIT of ONENESS**' reality!

This sounds like a **dream** that **we can make true**!
ALL rally forth with **best efforts** anew!
Each of us living must **decide to do**…
The next right thing that's **inside each of you**!

DO YOUR NEXT RIGHT THING!

Written for **ALL CHILDREN** and **ALL HUMANITY**,
by Donald W. C. Harris, December 15-18, 2009.

CONNECTION

ARE YOU IN A GANG...?

Are **you** in a gang that does no good?
Perhaps **someone** who's been misunderstood?
Then now's a good time to walk **ONENESS** wood
And think how to better **your** neighbourhood!

You can change **you** and do something worthwhile;
And even be happy...yes, laugh with a smile!
Tolerate difference! Make new **friendships** your style!
Break out of your clique! Start running **ONE**'s mile!

For **all** of **humanity**...not just a few...
For **each person** everywhere! Try something new!
Try spreading **your love**; it comes back to **you**!
You'll feel in **your gut**, what's right to do!

When **you**'ve done **your best, you**'ll feel better, **I**'m sure.
Go back to **gang members** with **your ideas pure**;
Show them **your secrets** for **peace** and **gang cure**...
You'll give **them** the **courage** to take the same tour!

Encourage **each person, themselves** to **love** first;
It then becomes easy to conquer the worst...
To let go of garbage...acquire new thirst
For **helping** out **others**...and make **ONENESS** burst!

Know that every move that **you** make,
Affects **us all**, like a giant earthquake!
So do **right things right**...for goodness sake...
To calm **OUR** waters in **OUR ONENESS** lake!

JOIN THE RIGHT GANG...
ONENESS INCLUDES ALL!

Written for better neighbourhoods everywhere for everyone,
By Donald W. C. Harris, September 15th, 2009.

BE ONLY YOU! NO DECOYS

Make the choice;
Have *your* voice!
Let no decoys
Disguise *truth,* "boys"!

Stay true to *self,*
And off the shelf.
Own your elf;
Be not of Delph…

I…will be me,
You too, can just be.
What comes, you'll see…
Can set us both free.

Let go *your* plan;
It's only of man…
(So out of hand).
We're *all God's* clan!

That other realm,
Will take the helm…
And overwhelm
All earthly qualm.

Let *Universe* guide
Your feelings inside;
Forget selfish pride…
Help *hearts* open wide!

ALL BE OF KIND HEART!

Written by Donald W.C. Harris, January
26th, 2008, for all to have heart.
Please show respect for, and be civil to all
citizens of the world. Thank you.

BLACK HOLE ONENESS

For three of four **forces**, they've opened the door;
Nuclear two...electro-magnetic one, is the score.
But gravity's still secret; we need to learn more...
Now, we think we know more than before!

Thanks to **Einstein**, **Hawking**, **Kaku**, and **Greene**,
And other scientists who contribute unseen,
With paper theories, academically keen...
Proof awaits collisions in Hadron Collider machine!

Maybe gravity seems so ultra-weak,
Because there's been some dimensional leak!
Usual 3-D viewing is not all that unique...
Eleven(or more)-D, hold truths that we seek!

Hawking's **Theory of Everything**,
May be found in Greene's evolved **M-string**.
It may turn out that **Quantum Physics** is king...
Particle **vibrations** make the whole **UNIVERSE** sing!

Thirteen point seven billion years ago,
Black hole **ONENESS**' dense **energy** let go...
Outward expansion from **big bang** and the glow;
Over time, the clusters of chaos still grow!

Proof of **Everything Theory**'s still a dream,
But when manifested, **GOD**'s magnificent scheme,
That links **ALL** things to **ONE energy** beam,
ALL's **ONENESS** will strengthen **HUMANITY**'s team!

WE'RE NOT THERE YET!

Written to honour those who pioneer discovery with integrity,
By Donald W. C. Harris, early April, 2009.

BONDS OF FRIENDSHIP

In bonds of friendship, I invest;
They're the ones that work out best.
Bonds with friends have waves that crest
From all directions: north, south, east and west.

Rebuilding trust can start with friends...
But don't stop there, do *self-extends;*
Reach out to those who need amen(d)s.
No enemies! That's what this message sends.

As **all** of **us** are part of **all others**,
Holding grudges in **selves** only smothers
The healing that **one** sends to **our brothers**.
Understand this, for the sake of **all mothers**.

Invest in bonds of friendship to bind **us all** together,
To complete **our** connection, despite any weather,
Like a big ball of twine, **orb** version of a tether;
Knowing **we** are **one** makes **us** tough as leather.

Examples that may teach that it's okay to hate,
Do no good among us...but create an evil state,
And soak **us** in pollution until **we** saturate.
Aren't hateful samples just misguided sucker bait?

So why not invest in a genuine friendship bond?
You'll find it really works, just like a magic wand.
Enjoy warm, fuzzy feelings **your** bonds will have spawned...
For **all our** earthly **beings** and those in realms beyond!

GO BEYOND; BEFRIEND ALL!

Written for all, especially Marlene, by Donald
W. C. Harris, April 26th, 2008.

FOREVER SUSTAINABLY RIGHT

Long term goals anyone has in sight,
Must be forever sustainably right!
Noble behaviour, each day, every night,
Is worth doing from startup, forthright!

Be honest, trustworthy, dependable, too;
Don't be a jerk! Be enlightened and true,
Sensitive, thoughtful, yes, be someone's glue!
Only your best can be expected from you.

If you make some mistakes along your way,
Don't be upset; learn from errors' sample tray,
With help from friends, and when you pray!
Nobody's perfect! That's what they say.

Ask for guidance, if ever in doubt;
Mistakes of others may help you out.
When you get it right, celebrate, shout!
Share your new knowledge! Spread it about!

Whatever you do, perform your best job;
You'll find in most cases, there's never a *prob;*
Sometimes, there may be soreness to swab.
Just fix it willingly; don't be a snob!

Every problem will have a solution,
And every dispute, its just resolution!
Nothing succeeds like **Source** institution;
Spirit uplifts way beyond diminution!

DO NOT RESIST!
SPIRITS ASSIST!

The above poem was written by Donald W.C. Harris 2010-09-02.

29

HOLD NO GRUDGES

Hold no grudges! Let them all go!
Move on this moment…on with your show!
First forgive, then, give love with a bow!
Get into now! Sink every free throw!

Each person's a player; each has a role.
Do more than your share! Help those on the dole!
Help them regain self esteem as their goal,
So they can help others discover their soul!

Look out for your neighbours! Look all around!
For sure you'll find one without feet on the ground.
For even one person, do something profound!
Help bring their life music…some heavenly sound!

When you give a hand to someone in need,
You do something right…you do a good deed!
You help mend a wound that may never bleed,
And start a good garden by planting **ONE**'s seed!

By helping just one, you've done what it takes.
You've spread goodwill, for **ALL**'s goodness sakes.
You've definitely raised all humanity's stakes.
You've shown high ethics! World conscience awakes!

Now, take care of gifts **GOD** gave us for free;
The rocks and soils, the life of the sea,
Splendid mountains, birds, bees, each precious tree,
The sky, the sun…and inner beauty of **WE!**

HELP ONE HELP ALL!

The above poem was written by Donald W.C. Harris 2010-11-19.

ME AND MY "WALKING HORSE"

My animal name, I've been told, is "**WALKING HORSE**";
I'm pleased with that name and have no remorse.
The spirits have named me and they're right, of course!
The code of my spirits is nothing like Morse.

The longer I hang out here on the Earth,
I sense that I'm called to spread joy and mirth
And get fuzzy feelings that signal rebirth.
The message is clearly abundance, not dearth.

"**WALKING HORSE**" is the name that just suits me;
Horse is an animal I'm so happy to be.
Through the eyes of "**WALKING HORSE**", I'll be able to see
More of everything through eternity.

It is the duty of "**WALKING HORSE**" now,
To comfort others and coach them how
To smooth out wrinkles from their weary brow;
To melt into **peace** with self and thou.

No matter what their trials may have been,
All persons are worthy of calm within,
Bliss that exudes beneath genuine grin
And supreme happiness without noise and din.

So I pray for the wisdom to master the art
Of guiding all others to play their right part,
To fast-track **kind conduct** as quick as a dart,
In order to foster **world conscience with heart**.

"WALKING HORSE" ASKS FOR YOUR HEARTFELT ACTIONS.

Written by Donald W. C. Harris, April 9th,
2008, in honour of "Standing Bear".

31

ONE CHOICE...ONE TEAM

We all must choose the winning side,
Or face a hugely downward slide.
Our **higher self** must be our guide...
Choosing right comes from inside!

If **we** veer from rightful path,
The risk is high for wrongful wrath.
Pray, keep **us** clean by spirit bath...
Cleanse away bad thoughts **one** hath!

There are no options for the choice,
For **fairness** has but one clear voice;
All the others...just background noise.
Go for good...then rejoice!

With **all** the **world** on just **one** team,
We'll stitch together **one** long seam;
We'll **all** have milk...and light rich cream;
We'll have it **all**...fulfill **our** dream!

We'll hold **one another** in **high esteem**,
And holding hands...walk any beam!
Every eye, with gleam extreme,
Will light the **UNIVERSE**'s **one** grand theme...

Of **life** for **ONE** and **love** for **ALL**,
Enough of both to keep **US** tall,
Feeling grand and never small...
Always in springtime...never in fall!

WE ALL PLAY ON THE
SAME TEAM...LET'S ALL WIN!

Written for all people, life and nature, by Donald
W. C. Harris, April 23rd, 2008.

TOUCH CONNECTION...THE FEEL OF WOMAN'S WOMB

There's no sense like touch,
That means quite as much...
Our connection by clutch
Bonds lives; **we** need this crutch!

Touch conveys its message clear...
Emotions warm or terrible fear;
A need for love or tender tear.
We all crave touch, my precious dear!

Newborns understand the feel
Of **woman**'s womb and vaginal keel,
That steers their path to their next meal,
Thence, on to master **life**'s turning wheel!

Our other senses give **us** clues,
To every aspect of all to dos.
Sight, sounds, smells and taste buds, too...
Together with touch, **all** empower **you**!

Touch ensures connection feedback.
Without the touch, **one**'s senses lack
Refined completion; the reins stay slack...
But **all together**, provide the knack!

And intuition comes into play;
That deep down feeling...it knows the way
To integrate **all** and action sway...
And make **us** wise in **our** display!

ALL HUMANITY...FEEL FOR ALL; USE ALL SENSES SENSIBLY!

Written for the sake of all human beings, by
Donald W. C. Harris, June 6th, 2008.

33

FRIENDSHIP

FIFTY YEARS

It's been fifty years since Bob and I met;
It's been a best friendship that ONE could ever get!
We both taught geology; helped many students set
Career paths in earth science, and beyond Earth, I bet!

I'm sure we both enjoyed working with the rocks,
Writing many papers and giving many talks;
We've carried heavy loads along our many walks,
And advised ourselves and others, on buying many stocks!

Some advice turned out wrong; some turned out okay!
No matter what we think we know, thinking goes astray!
Mankind doesn't know it all; it doesn't know the way!
Humanity must do better, starting now, today!

Throughout the years our wives and we
Have raised our families, but not for free!
Overall we like results we see;
We're contributing to our family tree!

I'm happy we still visit sometime,
While we are young and in our prime!
Though growing older is no crime,
Thinking younger feels so sublime!

BODIES MAY FADE;
SPIRIT MAKES THE GRADE!

The above poem was written by Donald W. C. Harris 2010-07-22.
It was written to honour a close and lasting friendship.

FOSSILMANIA

Palaeontology is not quite enough;
You've got to have fun mixed with learning stuff.
A twenty-first birthday is special, not guff.
Relaxing a little lets you cope with the rough!

I know you've got the party gear;
I saw you go for scotch and beer!
I know your friends will bring you cheer;
It's always good to have friends near!

Enjoy your time with friends and fam;
This day, let loose! There's no need to cram
Your head with facts for some exam!
Tonight you just won't give a damn!

I hope you have a super time.
You're still young and in your prime;
Your studies will help you earn your dime,
As palaeontologist with passion sublime!

You're working hard to make the grades;
Life's stage for learning never fades.
Keep eyes open and don't wear shades!
Geology's one of the most artful trades!

You're going to do what needs to be done;
You'll be the best at career number one!
I know you will, if you think it's fun,
'Cause love is key to all under the sun!

HAPPY 21ST BIRTHDAY, ALEXANDER!

The above poem was written by Donald W.C. Harris October 1st, 2010.
It was written for a great guy who is set on
becoming familiar with life of all ages.

HARMONIZE WORLD TONE

When it comes to **love**, you get what you give.
Hold on to **love** tightly and you won't fully **live**.
Keeping control means you rarely **forgive**.
Filter all thoughts through your **cardiac** sieve!

Soon you will see what remains in the strainer;
Let go thoughts gone through; it's a no-brainer!
Thoughts in the sieve will be your best trainer,
For blazing new trails to **new life** as a gainer!

With your head now cleared of all rotten debris,
And with new **Spirit wisdom** that will soon let you see
How best you can **better humanity**'s tree,
You can find **inner peace** and **sweet harmony!**

It does no one good to use violence or greed;
It's always **better** to **fulfill crucial need.**
Fights and wars spawn hate and make bleed,
Children of God, sprung from **God's ONENESS** seed!

Smooth the wrinkles in relations gone bad,
And restore all the **friendships** that you once had.
Go even further to make others **glad;**
Let them know **friendship** is more than a fad!

Friendship is one thing we all need to own;
Be friendly to all and **share** down to the bone,
So that not **one person** feels abandoned and alone.
Give it **our best** now! **Harmonize** world tone!

FRIENDS HAVE NO ENDS!

The above poem was written by Donald
W.C. Harris December 01, 2010.
It was written to spread friendship and peace to all.

ODE TO A COFFEE CUP

Harold felt badly when **my** cup **he** dropped.
He'd filled it with coffee; **my** cup **he** had topped...
But onto the floor, the coffee it slopped!
Harold cleaned up the floor as **he** mopped.

Harold confessed to **me**...cup pieces in hand
(This fine gift from **my son**, best in the land).
I read this **man**'s eyes, "**I**'m sorry; **I**'m damned!"
Forgive and let go...this mishap was unplanned!

Harold, **I** sense, is a kind-hearted **man**;
He feels for **others**...for **ALL**...without ban!
Harold's a credit to what **we** call **human**;
He's **my** new **friend**...and **part** of **ONE**'s plan!

He'll do worthy deeds for many a **person**,
To better **their lives**...not to dampen or worsen,
But to soothe **their** state; stop **them** from cursin'!
Harold's smooth ways keep **people**'s shirts on.

Harold's experience: chef for thirty-two years...
Somewhere in there, **he**'s had one or two beers!
His confident **nature**, always overcomes fears...
And makes **me** think **he**'ll have many careers!

Like counseling **others**; help **them** find **their way**...
And bring back **their will** to learn how to play!
"**Harold**, **I** wish **you** the best every day!
My friend, **you** are **worthy**...and truly **okay**!"

YOU ARE ONE!

ONE IS ALL! BLESS YOU!

Written for my friend, Harold Stewart, by
Donald W. C. Harris, June 15th, 2009.
"Harold, choose that your cup stays unbroken and always filled with goodness!"

SEEING SAMENESS

Befriending ALL, by befriending ONE...
That's how ONENESS gets begun!
Claim your spot in GOD's union;
Let ALL of us get ONENESS done!

Seeing sameness makes the difference!
Outward looks are fake appearance,
Giving rise to wrong inference,
Blocking much ONENESS experience!

ONENESS owns our commonness;
It sees inside us what to bless.
Forgive! Love! Help! Share! Caress!
These actions bring happiness,

And everlasting life of soul,
Fulfilled dreams in ONE's bowl,
Abundance all around the whole.
(Fishing's best above the shoal!)

Take a step towards doing right;
Ask for wisdom's best insight.
Find your peace! You'll sleep tight,
And never suffer, fear, or spite!

That's the beauty of ONENESS' plan,
For every woman and every man
Can easily wear ONENESS' tan,
Welcome ALL, to ONENESS clan!

IS IT HARD TO BEFRIEND AN ENEMY?
DO IT ANYWAY!

The above poem was written for all persons by
Donald W.C. Harris, March 07, 2010.

41

VOICE FROM THE DARK

The other night I forgot my house key;
I had arrived home late from a bingo spree!
It was very dark and past ten-thirty.
I knocked on the door quite loudly,

And hoped my wife would soon hear me;
I knocked once more, then again times three.
Knocking was not working, obviously!
A shrill voice from the dark called out to me…

The lady questioned, "Would my cell phone help?"
"Maybe", I answered, "First I'll try the doorbell;
That should waken her, though she does sleep well…
If not, I'll use your phone to break her sleeping spell!"

It wasn't too long before her shadow showed,
Behind the closed door where a fresh light glowed;
Then the door opened wide and her displeasure showed.
"I don't need your cell phone to lighten my load."

Another week went by and I'd thought a lot,
About that kind lady's offer to ease my spot.
I knew she was staying at the opposite house plot,
And vowed one day, I'd reward her **ONENESS** knot!

Another week slid by so fast,
Then I saw her outside in sunshine at last;
I ran out and met her; my thanks I cast;
New neighbours J. and J. are friends, not outcast!

ALWAYS INTEND
TO FIND A NEW FRIEND!

The above poem was written by Donald W.C. Harris 2010-08-03,
to promote friendship opportunities that
abundantly surround us; do not miss out!

HEALING

BEST HEALING...SPIRIT

The best **healing energy** comes from **SPIRIT**;
As channeled **vibration**, you may even hear it.
Powerful? Yes...but you need never fear it;
It comes with love and you need to be near it!

I let them operate inside of me...
Those **spirit doctors** of *"surgery"*.
Their **aura** merges with my **entity**,
Seeking my wellness with integrity.

I simply relax and let them go to it.
(How to mend me...is not mine to intuit)
In my quiet state, I know they will do it...
Carefully...I'm sure they'll get through it!

After awhile, when the experts have gone,
I'm certain of one thing...that I'll carry on,
Feeling better and better, in brain and in brawn...
Grateful for good health again, with each dawn!

I'm always so happy to know I am part
Of, not just my own, but of everyone's heart.
Spiritual healing gives a jump start
To each **ONE** and **ALL**...it's real **ONENESS** smart!

GOOD SPIRITS...EVERYONE!

Written For ASHA (Association of Spiritual Healers of Alberta)
by Donald W.C. Harris March 3, 2009.
Give thanks for the gift of healing!

45

DEPTH PERCEPTION

My **thoughts** and **prayers** go to you my **friend**,
To be with you tomorrow and time to the end!
I know you'll receive this message I send.
Healing prayers move fast just to **mend**!

At times one sees more when both eyes are closed!
Tonight you've one good eye; the other stays dozed;
Tomorrow the doctors your face will make *frozed*
And transfer a **donor's good eye** from…who knows?

Docs take out your bad eye and give you the new;
You don't care about colour: pink, yellow or blue,
'Cause all you're expecting is to **see out of two**,
With depth perception! What a grand new view!

You told me the docs will remove half your face,
And plastic surgery will fill up the space.
I know you'll be **blessed with God's hands of grace**,
And **while you are healing**, you'll discover new place,

As **one** who is **worthy** of **high self esteem**,
A **contributing member** of **Humanity's team**!
You'll see the **white light** of **God's energy beam**,
And all will be well as you **live** out **your dream**!

When I see you again at the hall where we play,
I'm sure you'll talk endlessly with so much to say!
Your **life** will move **forward** just like the **sun's ray**!
You will **be grateful**! You'll **thank God** every day!

ONE 3ᴿᴰ EYE 4 YOU
2 RESCUE ONE!

The above poem was written by Donald W.C. Harris 2010-10-20.
It was written **for David**, a good man with noble intent and
One who **sees Oneness** as **key** to **Peace**.

46

ENVISION FULFILMENT

Feel content with your imperfection,
And do not dwell on misperception
By other's expectations on inspection!
Just be happy with your own reflection!

No matter what discovery or detection
Of flaws or mistakes for possible correction,
Progress continues with resurrection;
Rest assured you have innate protection!

At times you think you may not be worthy;
That sets a stage for disease, such as scurvy.
Instead, believe you're attractive and curvy;
Set your mind on becoming daring and nervy.

Always beware of succumbing to stress,
And feeling overly squeezed by the press!
Know that coping success lies in how you address
The matters that seem to cause your distress!

Firmly believe that you're living your dreams;
Envision fulfilment with help from **spirit teams**!
Nothing will thwart any good-willed schemes,
And your balance is perfect on the highest of beams!

So relax and enjoy all that you do;
See only the good in all, through and through!
Capture the values from what's old and what's new;
You'll find peace of mind by just being you!

CALM IS THE BEST BALM!

The above poem was written by Donald W.C. Harris 2010-07-11.
It seeks to help bring good health, peace and
balance to all persons and societies.

FLOAT AWAY THE FLUFF

Float away the fluff!
It's all that bad stuff,
That makes life so rough.
Now, **you**'ve had enough!

Deal with **your** baggage!
That's all of **your** garbage,
In which **you** engage...
Keeps **you** locked in a cage!

Past **life** crap must go!
It's made progress slow...
Much more than **you** know,
It's prevented **your** glow!

Let go of **your** guilt!
It's like dirt and silt,
That's caused **you** to wilt...
You must be rebuilt!

Take hold and heal **self**!
Protect inner health;
Be no victim by stealth...
And **you**'ll know real wealth!

Stay true to **your** song!
Gut feels right! Go along.
Love helps **ALL** belong...
Love cannot be wrong!

Forgive **ALL** who're mean!
Pray **they** will come clean,
And shine with a sheen,
Like **ONE**'s never seen!

LOVE AND FORGIVE! LET GO AND LIVE!

The above poem was written for White Elk Medicine
Woman, by Donald W. C. Harris, May 10th, 2008.

FROSTY MIRACLE...

Four of us friends, three girls and a guy,
Gathered near Banff under cold wintry sky,
To ski thirty kilometers to cabin up high...
Day of fun was our plan; ...all went so awry!
We started at nine with spirits so free;
Midst beauty of mountains and trees scenery
Soon...there was one of us weaker than three,
Slowing group progress, Amanda, you see...
Was novice and ill equipped for such trip.
And it's not easy to say, "abandon ship!"
So, onward we pressed, with cold gaining grip;
Amanda, wet and freezing, started to flip.

Now too far advanced and no turning back,
Darkness had come and **all** looked so black;
Amanda and friend Anna would follow the track
Set by Nadia and Chris, seen by moonlight so slack.
A stream must be crossed no less than four times;
More wet and dark cold and more hills in our climbs,
Before we too, claim cabin's comforting grimes.
Now we're so close...we *hear* welcoming chimes.
Amanda has wanted to just fall asleep;
Hours she's been immobile and under the keep
Of Anna, who propelled both, to stand on her feet,
And to end this ordeal; make this a ***fait complete.***

Satellite radio, GPS and helicopter saved the day;
Hospital care will transform Amanda's fray...
And therein, still this young lady does lay.
There are lessons for all in this great team's play.

GOD SPEED YOUR RECOVERY AMANDA!

The above poem was written by Donald W.C. Harris,
Feb. 5, 2008 for those adventurers who enjoy the
outdoors. Respect Nature and properly prepare.

HEALING HEARTS

Circles of **friends** have no ends...
No sharp corners, just smooth bends...
No weak links...just strong **thought** trends
Of **ONENESS** only, where colour blends!

Where **good** and **healthy vibes** prevail;
Where astro-cruises can set sail;
Where **LOVE** for **ALL,** cannot pale,
And **SPIRIT**'s **healing** will not fail!

In **love-bound circles**' magic rings,
There can happen wondrous things!
Hear the **LIGHT** of **GOD**? It sings
PEACE to **ALL**! **Good health** it brings!

Connected circles of **positive thought**
Focus **healing POWER** we've each got;
This **SOURCE, THE FORCE,** cuts the Gordian knot...
Thus **ONENESS joins** every dot...

Of every spot in **ALL** that **is**!
SPIRIT has **answers** to every quiz,
And **healing hearts** is **SPIRIT** biz!
Join **ALL** dots...watch **circles** fizz!

SPIRITUAL HEALING CONNECTS!

The above poem was written on request, for the Association of
Spiritual Healers of Alberta, by Donald W.
C. Harris, October 31st, 2009.

HEALING POWER THAT REALLY MENDS

Casting blame just brings shame
To **SELF**; it makes **ONE** lame...
And sets relationships aflame;
Destroys the fun in any game!

Do not engage in this futile action!
Instead, help **OTHERS** find satisfaction...
Assist their load by less compaction;
Increase **LOVE**...multiply its fraction!

Make amends to all past friends!
Renew the **LOVE** that has frayed ends!
Understanding allows for bends...
HEALING POWER that really mends!

Live up to promises yet undone!
Doing this, means much to **ONE**...
And often can be done with fun.
Float out of cloud...into **SUN**!

If **YOU** still have a dream or two...
Get on with it! It's up to **YOU**!
Once **YOU** find your dream comes true,
YOU'll feel better...in fact, brand new!

Now **YOU**'re ready to make your mark...
By helping **OTHERS** find their spark!
Then **THEY**'ll emerge from dank and dark,
And climb aboard **OUR ONENESS** ark!

FLOAT WITH ME
ON ONENESS ARK!

The above poem was written for **ONE**...(which means for **ALL**)
by Donald W. C. Harris, May 30th, 2009.

IF YOU HAVE LOST SOMEONE

My friend lost his wife recently;
It was cancer that took her, indecently.
But now that she's gone, her spirit is free
To really start living victoriously!

Angels have welcomed her blessed soul
For focus on keeping the universe whole,
With all vibes in sync with the beat of **ONE**'s goal.
Light rays prevail in a world dark as coal!

Spiritual wisdom and knowledge supreme
Light up the way to everyone's dream.
By subtle shifts in **GOD**'s energy scheme,
Progress continues towards **ONENESS**' theme!

If you have lost someone dear to you,
Do not grieve for long; brighten your view.
Know that your dear one is still living too,
And will never die; believe that is true!

Now, get on with spreading the **LOVE** that it takes
To bring **ALL** together, for real, without fakes!
What are **WE** playing for? What are the stakes?
Sustaining **LOVE**'s world in **PEACE**…for **GOD**'s sakes!

SPREADING LOVE IS THE MESSAGE FROM ABOVE!

The above poem was written by Donald W.C. Harris 2010-04-11.
It was inspired by a comment in reference to the
passing of the wife of a new friend.

KEYS TO HEAL HER SON

I went walking yesterday;
A wee black dog met me half way.
Mid the road it wanted to play,
But there, we knew we should not stay.

To the sidewalk we both went,
Where a **pretty lady** on the cement,
Lifted the dog into her **kind arms** bent,
And started talking to me, a strange gent!

As our conversation moved along,
We sensed we were not strangers long.
She knew of my wife and had heard **Spirit**'s song.
We're really **neighbours** of **ONE faith** strong!

Her son, she said, has Crohn's disease.
The doctors and drugs haven't pleased
Her, so she's been searching **holistic** keys
To **heal her son** and to put him at ease!

She studies now, about **Spiritual "healers"**
And **organic nutrition**; she's put out her feelers.
I said, "My wife is church librarian, and a **"healer"**,
Reviewing books right now at home; you should see her!"

I left to walk; returned home; found the two ladies in talk!
I **pray** my new **friend** finds the **keys** to unlock
The **spiritual secrets** to reset her **son's clock**!
Hope is the **ONE** thing you really can't knock!

BE A GOOD FRIEND;
HELP NEIGHBOURS MEND!

The above poem was written by Donald W.C. Harris 2010-05-25.
It is dedicated to my neighbours across the road and down the hill.

ONE SONG

Why do **marriages** lose their gleam?
So quickly, many lose their steam,
And fall apart at **ONENESS'** seam!
What happens to that **noble team**?

Once there was a **joyful conjugal pair,**
A **trusted partnership, loyal** and **fair,**
Wherein each knew the other was there,
To **comfort, console,** and always **care.**

But **solidarity** started showing cracks;
Untold secrets hid some awful facts;
Infractions bleached their **common** wax!
Living together became worse than tax!

What started out as a **beautiful** thing,
Had rapidly crumbled and lost its spring.
No longer was there **ONE song** to sing,
As two broken **hearts** began to sting!

Trust was gone; the **marriage** doomed;
An ugly split o'er the duo loomed!
"Wait! **Our souls** can still be **rightly tuned**
By **Spirit healing,** we'll feel **immune!**"

"Let's **both forgive** and **right the wrong;**
We'll **pray** for **guidance** to make us **strong,**
And bring us back **our glorious ONE song!**"
ONENESS! It's **our best path** for **ALL life**long!

FORGIVE & LIVE...TOGETHER!
MAKE AMENDS! STAY FRIENDS!

The above poem was written by Donald W.C. Harris 2010-05-23.

PERSONS OUT THERE

Persons out there...with vacant stare,
Make me wonder, "Are they really aware?"
While they've been around most everywhere,
"Do they remember anywhere?"

Medications may have stripped them bare,
And left them feeling that they're just a spare;
And left them undone...thinking life's so unfair.
Their **life**'s been reduced; it hangs by a hair!

These **persons** held grudges, for too many years.
Bad thoughts harboured, brought on many tears,
And led to eternities of half-lives full of fears.
Not letting go, shuts down many gears!

But, with **spirit healing** and *"meds"* now in balance,
Lives have turned 'round; they're ready to prance!
Persons once lost, know their **lives** will enhance;
Enriched, they go forward...on with their dance!

There was a time, when these **persons** gave scare;
Now they have **hope**, without any glare.
Now, they are ready, to face any dare...
Knowing they'll make it, and not hold despair!

With faith in the **MAKER**, they know they're okay.
HIS guided path...it is the right way!
Know that no one's alone or at bay!
Together, **WE**'re **ONENESS** and not **ONE** is stray!

HOPE IS EVERYONE'S LIFE-LINE TO ALL!

Written for **every person,** by Donald W. C. Harris,
May 23rd, 2009. Note that an earlier, slightly different version,
under different title, had been composed, March 23rd, 2009.

REJECTION

Rejection can be so unkind;
The thought, alone, can stab the mind,
And sting like juice of lemon rind,
Or strangle like tight ropes that bind.

Rejection can cause one to cower;
To feel alone and without power;
And to let loose an anger so sour,
That one forgets to smell a flower.

It is a choice to feel rejected;
That is often what's expected.
But what if, maybe, one's elected
To make the choice to feel respected?

One's life is what one makes it...
So, if you want to fake it,
Believe that you can't take it.
Why not make your claim and stake it?

You've feelings of being unworthy;
That your world is topsy-turvy,
Like diseases worse than scurvy...
Act more for others; you'll feel free.

Become **ONE** with the flow;
Do your part of the show,
Of **ALL** on the go.
Forgive **ALL! GOD** will know!

ONENESS NEEDS YOU;
DON'T FEEL LEFT OUT!

The above poem was written by Donald W. C. Harris, Aug. 1ˢᵗ, 2008, for those who have not yet found their niche in the world of oneness.

RESTORE YOURSELF

Show yourself…every hole!
Expose the dregs of your soul,
Every dark zone, black as coal!
Understanding, that's the goal!

Hidden truths still locked inside,
Hold you back by thoughts you hide.
Alone, you chose not to confide;
Now, it's time to open wide!

Restore yourself! Become one whole!
Hold no more secrets in your bowl.
Some will listen and will console.
Not letting go, takes its toll!

Lay all your cards upon the table;
Free yourself…become more stable!
You can do it and become more able.
Forget what's past! It's now all fable!

You control the stuff you hold;
Kept too long it gets too old;
Pretty soon, it's growing mould,
Causing sickness that makes you fold!

Bent in pain, you can't think straight;
Before too long, it's way too late
To save yourself from an ugly fate!
Take action now, good friend; don't wait!

FEEL & HEAL, TO
ENJOY THE NEXT MEAL!

The above poem was written by Donald W.C. Harris, 2010-03-28.

SURGERY IS OVER

Your surgery is over; your day has gone well!
You say you have fears; send them to hell!
You must only love; that seems a hard sell!
You'll find inner peace that no fears can quell!

We know you miss your children at home;
They miss you too! You're the teeth in their comb!
They need your presence as model genome;
Children need moms (parents) like bubbles need foam!

In just a few days, you'll be with them again,
Though family and friends will still help, and then,
Because you are loved as chicks by their hen,
You'll know **God** loves all of his children! Amen!

Everything happens for right reasons unknown,
Though sometimes, issues seem quite overblown!
We worry! We forget **God**'s love we've been shown!
Each moment is right and one we all own!

It's hard, but imagine all is as intended:
Trials of one life all get extended
To all people everywhere, because we're all blended!
Nothing is separate! **God**'s love goes unended!

You will get mended; your soul will progress!
Your life will improve; you're already success!
Somehow you'll manage to master each mess!
You will be stronger; your soul **God** does bless!

LOVE'S HERE! LET FEAR CLEAR!

The above poem was written by Donald W.C. Harris 2010-11-10,11.

HUMANITY

ANYONE COULD BECOME DOWNTROD

There are no bad **souls**, just worn out foot soles!
A few bad breaks can put bodies on doles,
Then many awaken to near-empty bowls,
Their dreams and goals turned to debts and tolls!

And there but for the grace of **GOD**,
Anyone could become downtrod,
Whether close by or far abroad,
A few misfortunes can turn one's sod!

So count your blessings every day;
You won't miss them 'til they've gone away.
Enjoy your sunshine while making hay,
And just be grateful for freedom to pray!

Acts of **Nature** and mankind too,
Can sometimes be unkind to you,
And may end pain you're going through!
Be thankful you're alive to do

Helpful things for humanity's zoo;
Include: poor, sick, maimed and entire crew,
Of all the colours in our rainbow's hue;
Complete white light's energy glue!

Souls need never to be replaced!
Each **soul** remains eternally graced,
And chooses where it best be placed!
All **souls** are held in **GOD**'s embrace!

EACH SOUL IS WHOLE!

The above poem was written by Donald W. C. Harris 2010-08-04

COME OUT

Is someone squelching your ability,
Or questioning your stability?
Have you been shirking responsibility,
And dwelling on your irritability?

Maybe of late, you've taken to drinking,
Forgotten you're worth more than you're thinking;
Maybe with drugs, you've felt yourself sinking
Lower and lower; your money's red-inking?

These are good reasons to take a new look
At the way you've been living, in some shady nook.
Perhaps it's time for new recipes to cook;
Why don't you start to write a new book?

Come out of the darkroom you've been in too long;
Your brothers and sisters know you also belong.
You're part of world's purpose and humanity's throng!
Isn't it time to enjoy **ONENESS'** song?

No one needs to stay down in the dumps,
Alone in their garbage, crawling through clumps,
Traveling solo on roads with just bumps,
Or drowning in cesspools without any pumps!

Believe you still, can have all dreams come true,
By being yourself with the passion that's you!
By backing right acts and by changing your view,
Everything's possible! Take action! Just do!

TAKE JUST ONE BITE
TO TASTE THE LIGHT!

The above poem was written by Donald W.C. Harris 2010-08-27.

DOING "RIGHT", NOW

Impact the future by doing "**right**", now!
Our children depend on **us** to endow
Their world and make it **right** somehow!
Plant **right seeds** for **good fruits** on its bough!

A few bad apples can often cause rot,
And decay **good values** that **we've all got**,
So **do all you can**; hesitate not...
To **get rid of bad; make good count a lot**!

If **we all can love each other as kin**
(Which we truly are...under the skin),
Remarkable changes can then begin,
For **we're all the same**, deeply **within**!

Knowing that "**me**" **is** overall "**we**",
Can **help all persons** able to see,
Helping another is what **makes ONE free**,
For that is the root of **GOD's Essence Tree**!

Go now and make another **new friend**,
And **keep them forever**, for there is no end
To spreading the **message** that **GOD** wants to send...
We are all one! Make "**ONENESS**", **the trend**!

REALIZE ONENESS
AS KEY TO PEACE!

Written for all everywhere, by Donald W. C. Harris, January 26th, 2010.

ENDLESS SHADES

Twixt black and white are endless shades,
Of coloured strands in woven braids.
Blends of goodness with some spoiled grades,
Impact all through global trades!

With good and evil in most groups,
Good persons go through all the hoops
To serve the rest with multi-scoops,
Whilst they, in turn, look for loops!

If only all would do their fair bit
To deal with some of the extra shit,
If no one from their duty flit,
The entire world could benefit!

What if all pitched in fairly…?
If everyone got treated squarely?
Wouldn't all work out more merrily,
And friendships soar beyond just barely?

With many hands each load is lightened!
No one feels a noose get tightened.
Somehow sameness gets more brightened;
Difference fades and black gets whitened!

Under one common sun all are!
No one's entitled to inflict a scar
Upon a **being**, also **God**'s star!
Let's come together! Let's raise our bar!

JUST BEGIN! PITCH IN!

The above poem was written by Donald W.C. Harris 2010-10-10.
It was written for all human beings everywhere in the universe.

ETHICS HIGHER

With **ethics** higher, beyond the sky,
Send your **love** to **all** passersby!
While they may often wonder why,
You'll **know love**'s **right**, before you die!

Though some may view you as their enemy,
They may be **persons**, who need setting free,
From dogmas learned, unfortunately,
Like, "Hate thy neighbour's family tree!"

Of course, that path of teaching is wrong;
For it counters kind **humanity**'s song,
That calls for **ONENESS**, all time long,
To serve **GOD**'s **children**, **all ONE** throng!

So touch another, tenderly;
Know that **they** are part of **we**;
That **all** comprise **humanity**!
Talk! Agree! Set **mankind** free!

Peace, throughout the **universe**,
Is all that counts, in **ONENESS**' purse!
War is always the ultimate curse!
Let's all play at being nurse!

Take care of **others**, everywhere;
Consider **them** in daily **prayer**,
For **they** are **you-extensions**, there,
All precious **beings**, whose **souls** we **share**!

BE THERE, WITH LOVE TO SHARE!

The above poem was written by Donald W. C. Harris 2010-09-05.
It was written for all to know and have permanent
peace, no matter their dwelling.

GIVING BACK

Do something **worth-while to better** your world;
Whenever **you can**, let **your talents** unfurl!
Pick up a new spoon and give **your juices** a swirl!
Know **you'll do magic** for some **boy** or **girl**!

There are many **families** facing more and more debt;
Each passing day interest rates get upset:
It's not getting easier to necessities get!
Greedy scoundrels are **takers** who've **not paid forward yet**!

Giving back is the **good deed** that **needs to get done**,
By the crooks who have **cheated** for their **own selfish fun**!
A **billion poor people**, who too, **belong to ONE**,
Now **need to be rescued by rogues' caches** of bun!

When that's done, **ALL** and **ONE** will have won too!
That's because **each one of us is also part you**!
Every person must **do good** to **improve** the view,
For **ALL** on the **EARTH** and in the **Universe** stew!

Every person has something special to give;
Something to **help others improve how they live**!
Don't let **your GOD-given gifts** fall through the sieve!
Give them up freely! **Find your peace! Forgive**!

IF YOU'VE BEEN GREEDY, NOW HELP THE NEEDY!

The above poem was written by Donald W.C.
Harris 2010-12-13, in solitude
in a peaceful mountain cabin, to inspire those
persons who know they owe
humanity, to play fair: Finish your games! Make full restitution now!

HEART SMARTS

Heart energy fields can sense truth in ambience,
Before thoughts and knowledge of science
Influence and convince one's conscience.
Yes, **hearts** detect first any field interference!

Heart fields discover the future being made,
Well in advance of any future that's played,
Or any sod has been turned by the spade.
Heart sense protects one from the cutting blade!

Precise, concise instruction glows!
We cannot understand how this data flows;
Yet somehow, our **heart innately knows**
And warns us first, if an ill wind blows!

Long before we think to react,
Heart waves have already made their pact,
And caused us to assess total impact!
Heart smarts shelter us for **life**! That's fact!

Heart strings play their own sweet sound,
To guide us well above the ground;
When we **hear** their **harmonies** profound,
Noble rhythms of **heartbeats** pound!

Humanity's dignity depends on **hearts**,
That beat in sync with the universe parts,
Of **ONENESS LOVE** that just imparts
Heartfelt goodness! That's **heart smarts**!

HEART SENSE IS IMMENSE!

The above poem was written by Donald W.
C. Harris 2010-10-09, for all
persons everywhere to experience and practise more love and acceptance.

MIRROR CALLS

A mirror calls for ego's attention;
It shows pseudo "faults" by false pretension.
Do not be swayed by misapprehension.
Know **you're worthy**, and **meant for ascension**!

A mirror calls for true-self dissension;
Superficiality gives rise to high tension!
True worth is hidden and kept in suspension
Until the **inner source fills the missing dimension**!

Ignore outside temptations for your validation!
Spirit power inside you **can bring pure elation.**
Accept every motion of **internal vibration.**
It **comes with God's Force of ONENESS creation**!

Look into a mirror and you see your reflection…
An image, a form, wherein you perceive imperfection;
But that's not important for your **real worth introspection**,
That **swells deeply within** your **ONENESS reception**!

Abandon attachment to how others view you:
You know that no one has walked in your shoe.
There may be no reason to hang onto their view.
Trust in yourself for your very best cue!

Be **open to Spirit**, the **Power**, the **Source**.
For **intuitive wisdom**, adhere to **GOD**'s **course**.
Chart your **right paths** and have no remorse.
Let **ONENESS** guide you to the **ultimate bourse**!

TRUST IN MIRACLES…
NOT MIRROR CALLS!

Written by Donald W.C. Harris, February 19th, 2010, with hope that
all find and feel their inner peace, strength and confidence.

ONE WHOLE GRAIN

Generosity means so much!
It **helps fulfill our human touch**.
Treasures build inside **one**'s hutch,
By giving; let loose your clutch!

If you know someone's in a bind,
It will cost you little to **be kind**.
Ask **how you** can **ease their mind**?
Help some way! **Peace** you'll find!

Disregard class, race and **gender**;
Your loving deed will be **a mender**!
You needn't be a great big spender;
Be true to self, and always **tender**!

Love that bursts forth from your **soul**,
Means the **utmost to ONENESS' bowl**;
All of **us** must **pay** our toll!
Improve **HUMANITY**! That's the goal!

No one needs to go **without**,
For there's **abundance** all about!
GOD's **design** is **good**, no doubt,
So plan to **help each other** out!

When **none** are **desperate**, there's **peace**, not pain!
All people, then, can truly gain
Their **dignity**, without disdain...
Ready to **grow**, as **ONE whole grain**!

LET NONE BE DESPERATE!

The above poem was written for all people everywhere by
Donald W.C. Harris Feb., 2010 to recognize kind, generous
acts by family, friends, numerous others, even strangers. Bless
all your exemplary good behavior and benevolence.

PROPER VIEW

We all must take the proper view,
For there, but for the grace of **God**, go you!
Your turn may come to wear another's shoe;
Then, you'll know humiliation too!

Until, or unless, something goes very wrong,
You can't appreciate another's sad song!
If suddenly life pokes you with an ugly prong,
Your days and nights will seem awful and long!

And maybe then you will come to feel
For others suffering from a low-down deal,
Those uncertain of their next meal,
And those who move with only half a wheel!

No one knows when their turn may come,
To play the part of a homeless bum,
Roaming back alleys in some dangerous slum,
Bin-diving for bottles and any food crumb!

All live moments of ups and downs,
And try to smile to overcome frowns!
Whether in rural settings, cities or towns,
All battle thorns to reap a few crowns!

Once one has lived through some good and some bad,
One can appreciate the good once had!
Though some **human lives** have been ultra sad,
ONENESS LOVE can make **All** glad!

DO RENEW YOUR VIEW!

The above poem was written by Donald W.C. Harris 2010-11-18.

PURITY TALES

Who **I** am, should not matter;
I'm alive, so **I**'m a batter,
In this game of **life** in tatter.
Myths of purity...let **us** shatter!

Each of **us** is different and unique,
With gene pool mysteries quite antique;
No one can, with sureness speak,
Of heritage links without a leak.

Obsession with **one**'s purity tales,
Exclusive claims to holy grails;
These are ill paths...mistaken trails.
What good's a sailing ship sans sails?

It's **our** diversity that makes **us** strong;
Place faith in tolerance; position long;
Admit **we** know **we**'ve **all** been wrong
And **all** of **us** are of **ONE** throng!

I know within **my** heart, somehow
We'll make amends and jointly plough
Our fertile way to fruitful bough,
All together in **ONE** grand powwow!

WE ALL BELONG
ON THE SAME TEAM
IN THE GAME OF LIFE!
...Sky's the limit...

Written for all humanity, by Donald W. C. Harris, April 11th, 2008.

SIMPLE, SMART!

Always **keep it simple, smart!**
Do things right…right from the start!
Then, all proceeds fast, as a dart;
There is no horse behind the cart.

All goes well with **good intent**;
Even with all money spent,
Good emits its **worthy scent**,
And taps **the source** for all the rent!

Nothing stops a **vibe that's right**;
Its motions go on, day and night!
Results one thinks are out of sight,
Suddenly **shine bright** in rays of **light!**

So **focus** on what's **good for ALL**,
And never, ever, start a brawl!
What makes a person stand up tall?
Helping others not to fall!

So always **keep it simple, smart!**
Do things right, with all your **heart!**
Do it **now**; it's time to **start!**
Build ONENESS! Be ONE key part!

ALL TOGETHER is secret power;
Meet any challenge of any hour!
Reach the top of ONENESS' tower…
Enrich GOD's garden! Be ONE flower!

BE SIMPLY SMART;
BE ONE KEY PART!

Written for **PEACE for ALL,** by Donald
W. C. Harris, February 07, 2010.

U & I R 1

Hugs & kisses...kisses and hugs...
Are always better than misses and tugs;
Are always better than friction and "bugs",
To move ahead faster than slow moving slugs.

Your soul in a bowl is like horse without foal;
It's your duty to share to better the whole;
To spread all your good to fill up the hole;
To perk up the spirits of those on the dole.

It's the duty of each to help out the all.
By reaching to others, one grows very tall;
By teaming together, no-one will fall...
For all are linked on this blessed earth ball.

So go do your part to carry our load;
Make it better for others while they're down on the road.
The Earth is our home...a generous abode
You are so vital...a functional node.

BLESS OUR WORLD...AND
ALL THAT IT IS!

Written for all on June 16, 2007, by Donald W. C. Harris,
who believes in hope, and that we can, and will, do whatever it takes.

UNIVERSE NEW

The bottom billion...poverty struck!
How do **they** cope? Are **they** stuck in muck?
Do **they** crawl through garbage, goop and guck?
Do **all** these **persons** feel down on **their** luck?

These questions, **ALL** must contemplate.
How come it is **theirs**...and not **OUR** fate?
When is it time for **ALL** to feel great?
What can **WE** do...before it's too late?

As **I** gaze skyward through the trees,
I pray to **GOD** on both of **my** knees.
I'm warm in the sun; **I**'m cooled by a breeze...
I'm grateful now; the moment **I** seize!

It is fair to take, while a living **you** make...
But giving back is what's always at stake!
Each is just here for **another**'s sake!
ALL has the power to make **OUR EARTH** quake!

Don't feel self pity or hard done by...
That pseudo-escape is one giant lie.
Instead, let it go! Here's a good reason why;
Contribution is truly **each person**'s best buy!

OUR ONENESS CLUB needs **me** and **you**.
It is the way...but with much left to do,
To help make the **WORLD**, a **UNIVERSE** new...
That's kind to **ALL**...not merely a few!

ONENESS CLUB IS FOR ALL!

Written for **ALL** to enjoy the **abundance** of a
sustainable UNIVERSE, by Donald W. C. Harris, June 13th, 2009.

WE ARE MUCH MORE

We are much more than what we do.
What we do gives but one clue…
The merest glimpse of what turns our screw;
A lonely spice in our complex stew!

What we do leaves so much more
To be discovered behind closed door.
Learn inner core for our total score!
See all potential! Do not ignore

The skills and talents buried deep inside,
Where spiritual wealth does reside!
Look closely; surf your swelling tide;
Hop aboard a different ride!

Discover more about your real being;
There's so much more than what we're seeing!
Give some other calling meaning!
Know self! Show self! Be revealing!

No one can know another's scope,
Nor can one feel another's hope,
Or sense one's hanging from a rope!
Is it enough to barely cope?

Get more from life! Diversify!
You'll never know, until you try.
Go deep inside to reach your sky!
Otherwise, just wonder why.

JUDGE NOT ANOTHER!
ACTUATE INNATE GIFTS!

The above poem was written by Donald W.C. Harris, 2010-04-12.
It was written to spur discovery and expression of potential gifts,
skills and talents which currently lie beyond present awareness.

WHEN ALL IS RIGHT

Aborted foetus, unwanted child,
Conceived in special moment wild!
Excited semen, one egg beguiled,
And your unlucky number was dialed!

We know your soul will try again
To make its journey to earth's plane.
Its efforts will not ever wane,
Nor will they always be in vane!

Eventually, when all is right,
You'll choose parents not uptight,
Who, will want to **love** your **light**,
And cherish you with all their might!

You will grow up spreading **love**,
Without hate, and give hate a shove!
Embrace all in **Heaven**'s glove!
Nothing stops **ONE**'s **PEACE** dove!

Only **love** can bring salvation
To every person in every nation.
When all hum only **ONE**'s vibration,
That's **WORLD PEACE** harmonization!

ONE'S VOICE UNITES
ALL DIFFERENCE!

The above poem was written by Donald W.C. Harris 2010-04-13.
It was written for peace for all to enjoy throughout all space, forever.

WITHOUT LOVE

Obsessive greed will keep you poor;
Possessive greed is evil's lure
To make you think you lack **love** pure.
Without true **love**, there'll be no cure!

Your **life** may fill with stuff and toys,
But all those things are simply ploys,
That keep you sad; they're just decoys
For what brings **happiness** and **joys**!

You thought you needed full control
Of everything within your bowl,
Of everyone; that was your goal,
But one can't own another's **soul**!

To free yourself from apparent lack,
You've got to start by **giving** back;
Help out others! Take up slack!
With **kindness**, soon you'll have the knack!

It won't be long before you'll know
That all your stuff was worthless show;
Pointless trash you had to stow! **Let go**!
Control can strike a nasty blow!

With all your crap now gone from site,
You'll have no need to bark or bite,
Downgrade others, or start a fight!
Now you're doing what is right!
Peace has found you! Hold on tight
To **ONENESS, GOD**'s white light!

GROW AWAY FROM GREED! PLANT THAT SEED TO HELP ANOTHER'S NEED!

The above poem was written by Donald W.C. Harris 2010-o5-23.

LOVE

A VALENTINE'S A SWEETHEART

A valentine's a sweetheart;
Would **YOU** please be mine?
It's part of **GOD's design,**
ALL HEART-STRINGS entwine.

No matter what **YOUR thoughts** are...
OUR thoughts will be as **ONE!**
Together, WE'll be **stronger,**
And have a lot **more fun.**

So let the **good things happen...**
Not just for **YOU** and **I.**
Let **ONE** and **ALL** and **EVERYONE...**
Know LOVE, and **never die.**

Once **EVERYONE** has **found LOVE...**
All **WORLDS** at **PEACE will be,**
For that's **the BLESSING from above,**
For **ALL WORLDS** to **be free!**

SHOW ONLY LOVE FOR ALL!

Written by Donald W. C. Harris, February 13, 2005.
Amended February 13, 2008 and February 14, 2010.

ALL LOOKING FOR AFFECTION

We are all looking for affection;
When found, it brightens our complexion.
It gives us good feelings near perfection,
And comforts...on deep introspection.

We all have great need to know love;
Love is so much better than an *off-shove*,
Love spawns a gentle image of the peace dove.
Love's a special gift from heaven above!

There is nothing that means more to us,
Than someone making loving fuss.
This helps us to ignore all worldly muss,
While returning affection in surplus.

Existing without someone's loving care,
Is like living with all one's cupboards bare;
One views the world with empty vacant stare.
Love will come to all through faith and prayer!

Give someone your love every day;
Show them you care in a special way;
Do it now, dear friend, without delay!
Some love will cycle back to you to stay!

No one's ever weak by show of compassion;
Acts of caring, will soon set all the fashion...
When that happens, we'll have sufficient passion,
To reach that magic level, with nothing to clash on!

DO IT NOW...SHOW SOMEONE
YOU LOVE THEM!

Written with all in mind, by Donald W. C. Harris, April 24th, 2008.

ARE YOU INTO ME?

Are you into me like I'm into you?
Doing desires only lovers would do?
If you're into me like I'm into you,
The world is our oyster and we are the stew.

If you're into anything daring or not...
Then you are my bloodstream...never to clot!
My heartbeat, my sunlight, my every deep thought.
You're all that I am; all the meaning I got.

Are you needing me like I'm needing you?
Are we both in a quandary with nary a clue?
Together our souls can strengthen our brew...
And keep us in shape without even a *flu*.

Without you my darling, what path would I take?
Rudderly worthless...I'd be truly a fake...
Adrift on wild ocean...not calm on a lake...
So believe in me always, I plead, for God's sake!

Written by Donald W. C. Harris, June 2007.

GARDEN OF GOOD

"I think, therefore I am!", or...
I don't think, therefore I am more!
Which, I wonder, really opens my door?
Which, I wonder, frees my spirit to soar?

So far, my thinking has not served me well;
My thoughts have only made my head swell,
By bouncing around in my skull prison cell...
Much noise...I'm confused; feel like hell! Can't you tell?

I'm often too much inside of my head;
Maybe, it's better to let go instead;
To quiet my mind...pretend I'm in bed;
Imagine bright spectrum from violet through red.

I see the white light coming in from above...
I sense it stream through me; there's peace and white dove.
I'm in tune; I feel comfort; I'm so full of love!
I can soak up the good stuff; give bad stuff a shove!

Now all should be open for pure energy flow,
To become a new person with no baggage in tow.
Blessed seeds from the Universe can take hold and then grow,
In my garden of good, where there's no lawn to mow!

WHAT'S IN YOUR GARDEN?
IS IT TIME TO REPLANT?

Written by Donald W. C. Harris, April 09th, 2008
with hope for a global garden of good.

ONLY LOVE

Owning nothing makes **ONE** rich!
Owning things can make one a bitch!
Ownership has one big glitch…
Possessive greed! That's the hitch!

If one owns nothing, **ONE** is richer!
Then one can see a bigger picture,
Of what's important in the mixture;
One is more than just a fixture!

One can do for others too;
Give a helping hand, or two!
Lose that awful urge to sue!
Befriend all, not just a few!

Imagine how the world could be,
If every debt could be wiped free,
High stress could lower instantly,
No dirty deeds done desperately!

The world could be a better place;
Nearer heaven, by **GOD**'s grace!
There is no need for war or mace;
Nor any other human disgrace!

No need to hate a 'different' race!
Lock all evil in a sturdy case;
Let us all, good things embrace;
Let's only love every face!

'NOTHING' MAKES SENSE!

The above poem was written by Donald W. C. Harris 2010-05-23.
It was written for all people to improve life for all persons
by more compassionate, respectful and decent behaviour.

SYMPHONY OF ONENESS

Symphony of **ONENESS**...your sweet music fills my ears
With messages more meaningful than diamonds from DeBeers.
Your melodies bring harmonies; the air around me clears.
Magically, your theme of **LOVE**, eliminates all fears!

Symphony of **ONENESS**, please play your **loving** sound,
So long lost **souls** upon the earth can quickly be re-found;
So those who wander aimlessly, no longer pavement pound,
But find their **peace** on **nature**'s trails where **heaven**'s sounds abound.

Conductor **GOD**, oh! gracious **ONE**, **YOU**'ve ably synthesized
All noise patterns of the **universe**, so intricately comprised.
Too bad so many **persons** have been desensitized,
And have not heard a single word and missed your noble prize!

Restore to them their hearing that they may know the joy
Of **LOVE** without fear, they knew as newborn girl or boy.
Reawaken their awareness of the **power** of your toy,
To help them know **YOUR LOVE** as **ONE**'s new employee.

Keep right on orchestrating all **YOUR ONENESS** tunes!
They inspire us to **LOVE ALL PERSONS**, even **our** buffoons!
YOUR songs spread **LOVE** afar, as in giant **PEACE** balloons,
So **ALL persons** and **all nations** hum like **OM**'s bassoons.

When all that happens, **ALL** of **US**, can really celebrate,
Knowing that **OUR ONENESS** has reached a whole sum state!
When **each** of **us** hugs **everyone**, as **loving soul** and mate.
Together, **ONENESS** symphony, **we** with **GOD**, do orchestrate!

HEAR THE HARMONIES
OF ONENESS SYMPHONY!

Written for the ears of **ALL PERSONS** everywhere,
By Donald W. C. Harris, October 7th, 2009.

TAKING YOU TO PARADISE

If I pass over before you do,
Will you recall the "hell" I put you through,
Or only the good times we shared as two?
I'll know you'll still **love** me as I'll still **love** you!

Though many deep **feelings** will remain unexpressed,
I'll know we've both **loved** and gave **life** our best,
In spite of **life**'s trials that faced us in test.
I **loved** those **sweetest moments** when we gently **caressed**!

If you move across before I leave **Earth's plane**,
Though the **sun** may shine here, I may still **sense** some rain.
If you do go on over, I'll remember your pain,
Until we're both in **Heaven** where we'll **love** once again!

I've often had **dreams** of taking you to **paradise**;
So far, we have **tasted** just one very small slice.
Still, I **dream** ahead to that time when we'll splice
All our strands together by some **ONENESS** device!

Has anything been missing from our **unity**?
Our **friendship** and **love** give **opportunity**,
And surely bolster our immunity,
So nothing threatens our impunity!

WE TWO ARE ONE!
NOW LET'S HAVE FUN!

The above poem was written by Donald W.
C. Harris in early August, 2010.

NATURE

CANMORE'S PEAKS

High picturesque mountains, peak after peak,
Comprise Canmore's Rockies all looking sleek.
This splendid scenery is singly unique;
It's been here for ages: Alberta's geo-antique!

In winter, these peaks are whitened with snow,
Though steep rocky slopes have some grey for show.
If overhead clouds stay still, winds don't blow;
When it is windy, cloud shapes change and flow!

More and more evergreens colour the slopes,
As down below tree-line life more than copes!
People in Canmore are bright with new hopes;
Dreams have grown beyond coal-mines and stopes!

When snow has subsided and daylight lasts longer,
Sounds of all life get louder and stronger.
Thoughts of lifelessness couldn't be wronger!
Sluggish animals come alive to ease hunger!

Rainbows of colours take over the meadows,
Enriched by flowers in fields and in rows,
And by many a plant that naturally grows.
All life is nourished by clean watery flows!

It's so awesomely peaceful in this wilderness,
In my rustic chalet away from bustle of business!
Away from the city I know more comes with less!
Keeping life simple is best, I confess!

WILDERNESS PEACE
BRINGS STRESS RELEASE!

The above poem was written by Donald W. C. Harris 2010-12-13.
It was written in a private resort chalet in the
peaceful mountain environs of Canmore.

DANDELIONS...NOT JUST WEEDS

Dandelions are **flowers** too,
Not just weeds through and through!
Their **golden** hue adds to the view
Of **green** fields after morning dew!

Beneath bright skies of brilliant blue,
What's more **fun** for "**kids**" to do
Than picnic in a **yellow zoo,**
With **dogs** and **cats,** and **wild things** too?

Fields of '**lions and buffalo beans,**
Look good on **grasses** and other **greens;**
They really make such **beautiful scenes.**
No one should care about stains on jeans!

Dandelions make a **tasty wine;**
Their roots can make **coffee fine;**
Bees visit '**lion flowers** to dine
On what must be their **gold mine!**

Some **city folk** attending lawns of grass,
Dig or poison 'lions en masse;
They **waste life,** as the hours pass!
No doubt they think I'm a stupid ass!

But **dandelions have rights,** you know;
They have **purpose,** so **let them grow.**
Should we be judge of what seeds blow?
I think not. My answer is, "**No**".

NATURE KNOWS
WHY EVERYTHING GROWS!

The above poem was written by Donald W. C. Harris 2010-05-25.
It is a tribute and a warning to respect the beauty,
the power, and the balance of nature.

DOLPHINS, TURTLES AND OIL

Dolphins, turtles and oil in the bay,
Shrimp, and fish and some birds of prey,
Have all come together in this month of May,
Which **life** will remember as 'Waterloo' *day*!

The wetlands near shore, all drenched in oil,
Now face the chore: learn fast not to spoil!
Tempers are flaring, their juices aboil!
The President is there, pledging recoil!

Deep water drilling is risky at best,
Even when all is prepared for the test!
This time 'success' really has messed;
No one envisioned…far worse than Valdez!

Pray for the well to be soon, safely plugged.
High pressure oil/gas is stifled when slugged
By heavy mud/junk that slows its flow, as if mugged.
Rising fluids bog down; when cement sets, they're jugged!

Much life has been lost from the oil debris.
Volunteers will clean some, then, set the few free;
When an accident such as this tragedy
Occurs, renewal fails! We need **ONENESS**' strategy!

As we move forward with good intent,
And maximum caution, care and consent,
Bulldozer mentality, that's all hellbent,
Has no place in what we implement!

PRAY 'WATERLOO' DAY
WILL GO AWAY!

The above poem was written by Donald W. C. Harris 2010-05-28.

FIVE HUNDRED DUCKS

Five hundred **ducks** stuck in a toxic **pond**;
Their deadly warning lack...no canon sound.
Oil **personnel** waved their magic wand-
Bad weather's the reason the **birds** were conned!

Only five of five hundred they say might be saved.
All of the **others** have been subtly betrayed.
The best of plans had just been delayed...
Had the canons fired, no **birds** would have stayed!

So much for plans that seem ready made;
Even the best of some plans that are laid,
Pale when they fail and away they fade.
All threads of **life** weave a delicate braid!

The **birds** aren't alone in **NATURE**'s balance;
We too, are impacted when **they** take a chance.
Mistakes can be costly and don't **life** enhance.
Life wants to dance...not be pierced by a lance!

No **one** intended for those **ducks** to die...
But **we**'re not yet masters of **earth** and **sky**.
Is it not time to slow down and ask why?
Why do **we** hurry to make **us all** cry?

There's more than rush in our **ONENESS UNIVERSE**;
Think of **all** outcomes of **our** doings diverse.
Make this **our** duty...don't destroy or disperse...
Be **NATURE'S steward**, its **doctor**, its **nurse**!

RESPECT ALL LIFE'S MEANING AND WORTH!

Written for all and the preservation of the universe,
by Donald W. C. Harris, April 30th, 2008.

FOR BEST SUCCESS

If **you** were fond
Of stuck **ducks** in a pond,
You'll know they were conned;
You'll know they were pawned!

Oil production from tarry sands...
The very idea stimulates glands;
But the process demands
Put such stress on the **lands**!

Talus pond spills and toxic leaks,
Contaminate **air**, the **soil** and **creeks**,
And likely alter **birds** and their beaks.
Life downstream...it's the bleakest of bleaks!

Is greed at the core of what **we** speak?
Is it just dollars that **ALL** should seek?
Careless acts make **ONE** into a geek,
Competing with **others**, clique against clique!

World **energy** sources are all around;
In **atoms**, the **sun** and **wind** it is found;
Geothermal is best...it's **heat** in the ground
Is always available! **Earth**'s **heat** is so sound!

Don't get **me** wrong...**I**'m not against progress.
Stop making a mess! Do better! Do more with less!
Use **NATURE** wisely for best success...
Not by stampede, but by gentle caress!

USE GOD'S GIFTS WISELY!

Written by Donald W. C. Harris, May 4th, 2008,
in remembrance of human errors that sacrificed life.

GEM OF WESTERN CANADA, EH!

It's a beautiful day and I'm driving west,
Across the plains to where the views are best.
I've reached the foothills with their rolling crests,
Just beyond soar the peaks that will end my quest!

There's Mount Yamnuska, just ahead to the right:
The sleeping giant's cliff face, brown-yellow bright,
Juts vertically upward into sky's sunlight
And rises from dark scree, just below and in sight.

But the real mountain gem that I'm heading for,
Has secluded chalets that I just can't ignore;
This haven up the hill from the Bow's valley floor,
Is so naturally beautiful with treasures galore!

Now I'm out on the deck of my rustic chalet;
The warm sun is shining; it's a splendid day;
All around are the peaks, trees and rocks on display.
This is truly the **gem of western Canada**, eh!

This resort setting is **Mother Nature**'s supreme;
It's enough to fulfill **One**'s ultimate dream!
Bow valley's **waters** bring **life** with its stream.
Nothing can top this resort's fabulous team!

Spirit power pervades all and won't cease;
Let it be yours and forever increase;
Remember to **love** to set your release;
No matter the setting, we all can find **peace**!

EFFECT RESPECT!

The above poem was written by Donald W. C. Harris 2010-08-25.
It was written in reverence to a special spot.

MOTHER EARTH...
WIN HER PRIZE!

Mother Earth...she is so wise!
When she talks, don't roll your eyes.
Her wisdom may come in disguise;
Listen closely...win her prize!

Smell her fragrant scents in air;
Learn lots from them, everywhere!
Caution! Some are to beware;
While others may be, oh, so rare.

Tasting nature can offer clues,
As valuable as your mindsets choose.
Treasures are missed...if you lose...
Don't dull your senses with numbing booze!

All around you is beauty to see;
It's there in every you...and me...
Every mountain, every tree, every bird, every bee.
With eyes closed...all visions are free!

Feel the warmth from dreams you chase;
They comfort, like silk and lace...
And help you wear any brand new face...
Feel empowered! Meet challenge with grace!

YOU CAN DO ANYTHING!

Written to alert others to their infinite potentials in the world of
Superabundance that God has given for all to appreciate...by
Donald W. C. Harris, on Canada's Labour Day, September 1st, 2008.

OUT OF TIME

We need to revisit our concept of time;
The clocks we live by, have stolen our prime;
With focus diverted toward settings of crime,
We stifled progress toward life more sublime.

We all feel pressures of deadlines imposed;
Best outcomes don't happen with chakra closed!
Spirit flows freely when relaxed and composed!
Solution comes easily, once problem's diagnosed!

We deal with straight-line time, in man-made clocks...
Some are distinguished with their ticks and their tocks;
Timing devices control the pace of all walks;
And counter natural cycles in what really rocks!

Natural rhythms of the universe have periodic repetitions...
Meaningful events, which influence life conditions.
For instance, lunar cycles, woo reproductive exhibitions,
And seasonal adjustments prompt nomadic expeditions.

Man-made time has served a purpose...
But soon it may entirely usurp us.
We've speed-of-life in massive surplus.
Slow down...before the spin can burp us!

Let's back off! Step down from convention!
Get back to moon rhythm! Look at Mayan time invention!
See signs of natural rhythms! See more than one dimension!
Use **God**'s gifts wisely! We can rise to peak ascension!

EVERYTHING IN TIME...
NATURALLY RHYTHMIC!

Written in the nick of time, for all persons,
by Donald W. C. Harris, May 25th, 2009.

PRESERVATION FARMING

All of **us** must farmers be,
And stewards of all forestry,
Protectors of **all life** at sea,
That is, saviours of biology!

No one has a right to rape
A person, ocean, or landscape;
Or to pollute or contaminate,
Abuse or bully or worse yet, hate!

Though **each person** has unique
Potential to reach one's peak,
Humanity thrives on collective squeak;
Together, let our **ONENESS** speak

Of only **love** and **good** for **all**,
Fairness, trust and freedom tall.
No one's allowed to drop its ball;
That way, our **ONENESS** cannot fall!

ONENESS is our only way,
For every one to have a say;
And to be sure of just, fair play,
And skies stay blue, never grey!

HARVEST WITH CARE;
ABUNDANCE IS TO SHARE!

The above poem was written by Donald W. C. Harris 2010-08-15.
It was written for all life everywhere.

QUAKES AND TSUNAMIS

Earthquakes and tsunamis…some giant, some small,
Can bring dark devastation, fearful life to a crawl,
Cracked highways, broken bridges and buildings that fall;
People panic! Near death…and dying, some writhe by a wall!

A big quake, when it hits, breaks things to bits,
By shaking and shearing, until crumbling quits.
All that's around just trembles…then splits!
Not a thing stays intact; all goes to shits!

No one can fathom a quake's energy released!
When earth quakes at depth, vibration's increased;
Breaks in earth's crust allow stress to cease,
As rocks fold…then snap, to take on a new lease!

When plate tectonics change bottoms of oceans,
Waves adopt quake power with enormous devotions;
They morph into huge waves with **divine** emotions,
Then cross **THE ONE OCEAN**…and cause great commotions!

Giant tsunami waves on the seas,
Wreak total havoc; they do as they please,
While wiping out beaches, resorts, huts and trees.
Shoreline populations go down…on their knees!

MOTHER NATURE's in power; she shapes evolution…
Of life, of things, and **HUMANITY**'s 'solution';
Our influence seems to be suffering dilution,
So, let's **ALL** strive more for **ONENESS resolution**!

ALL IS UNFOLDING
NATURALLY!

Written by Donald W. C. Harris, February 27, 2010, for **ALL** to benefit.

QUAKING ACTION

There's a stench of death and putrefaction!
It's been five days since quaking action;
Millions wander, desperate for traction!
Hungry, thirsty, midst rubbly compaction!

Flimsy structures, now mostly crumbled,
Include even palaces; they too have tumbled!
Under debris, screams for help have been mumbled;
A lucky few have been freed and have stumbled!

Assistance arrives from afar every day,
To try to make sense of disordered array.
There aren't any children happy at play!
If any had choice, would even one stay?

With food and clean water suddenly rare,
Human behaviour sparks to irrational flare;
And people do things they never would dare!
Faced with tough choices, does one still do what's fair?

To restore some order where so much is destroyed,
Requires resources and humans deployed,
To uplift the spirits so hopes can be buoyed!
Can tragedy hide blessings subtly decoyed?

Remind all the people that we are all one;
That not one is isolated under the sun!
Each has a duty, until all has been done,
To brighten the life of even just ONE!

COUNT YOUR BLESSINGS!
VIEW WITH RIGHT PERSPECTIVE!

Written in remembrance of the Haitian earthquake of January 12, 2010,
by Donald W. C. Harris, January 17, 2010.

SIMPLE THINGS

Another day has come my way...
I get another chance to play;
Another chance to have my say.
I wonder what I'll do today?

I must acknowledge simple things...
Like **sun** that warms and **voice** that sings;
Like **water** coming from the **ground** in **springs**;
Like humming **birds** with special **wings**!

I must give thanks for **children**, too...
They are the **force** to get **ONE** through;
Our **animal friends** of earthly zoo,
Have proven loyalty, tried and true.

The simple **plants** and giant **trees**...
They give **us life** and shelter **bees**;
The lofty **mountains** with rocky screes,
Provide the **peace** that **all** can seize.

Fresh **air** to breathe...that smells so good,
With **flower** perfumes and essence of **wood**;
These **blessings** are free...rich **soul food**.
Respect them always! Understood?

Now let me see...what else is there?
Oh yes...soft **beauty** of my true **love**'s **hair**;
And, of course, the **UNIVERSE** everywhere...
My **source** of **power**! I've not a care.

GIVE THANKS FOR SIMPLE THINGS... THEY'RE YOUR FREE SOURCE OF POWER!

Written by Donald W. C. Harris, July 13th, 2008, in
appreciation of all that the universe provides.

SUBTLE SIGNS

Animals know when it's time to go;
They sense vibrations to and fro,
Long before human beings know,
Before tsunamis and storm winds blow!

Humans ignore the subtlest signs,
While other animals make bee-lines,
Before earth shakes like exploding mines,
Breaking boats and ripping vines,
Displacing hips and twisting spines!

Cats and dogs, turtles and frogs,
Chickens and cows, bees and hogs,
Even slugs hidden under logs,
Sense traces of tremors in sun or in fogs!

People must have too much in mind,
To pay any heed to clues they don't find;
Or maybe their brains have numbed or resigned;
Many have acted like their brains are blind!

All of a sudden, the sea rushes in;
Huge waves catch some people having to swim
For their lives! Ocean force depends on **HIM**!
It swallows the shore and all that's within!

Any that headed, with animals, higher
And out of harm's way to a safety outlier,
May yet get to fulfill their lifetime desire!
Believe in animals' connected hot wire!

ANIMALS KNOW WHEN TO GO!

The above poem was written by Donald W. C. Harris 2010-07-20.
It was written with respect for all life and natural events everywhere.
A special feeling goes out to a friend and her elderly cat, Gremlin.

SUMMER SUN FUN

Summer's now with us; bring on summer sun!
Summertime's a great season for good family fun,
Together! Company is better than lonely as one,
So invite friends and relatives; just get it done!

Go out for walks; breathe summery fresh air;
Feel summer's warm comfort everywhere.
Sun puts all at ease, without worry or care,
And makes one feel wealthy in a land that is fair!

By absorbing the heat and free scents all about,
We're like collection plates, without any doubt,
And even like tea pots with a magical spout,
Refreshing one's chi and healing one's gout!

Summer surrounds us with beauty and peace,
So go for a walk to let anger release!
Fuse feelings with flowers to sense an increase
In awareness, of summer's birdsongs and bees!

Be grateful for all the free good things around,
From trees in a park to soils in the ground,
And all the sweet songs that make up Earth's sound…
Melodies, harmonies, spirit's vibes so profound!

No one lives fully without tasting some fruit;
All know it's wrong to pollute and pollute,
Or be hurt and bullied by some big galoot!
Make friends with summer; make this one a beaut!

SUMMER IGNITES
ONE'S SO*U*LAR LIGHTS!

The above poem was written by Donald W.C. Harris 2010-06-23.
It was written at the request of West Hillhurst Go-Getters.

SYNOPSIS: EVOLUTION OF OCEAN, LAND, AIR AND LIFE

Without **THE ONE OCEAN**, there'd be only **THE ONE LAND**!
Drain away **THE WATER**; there'd be just **ROCK** and **SAND**,
Magnificent **mountains**, and **valleys** ultra-grand!
Celebrate this **ONENESS**! Strike up the band!

The dried out **EARTH's CRUST** opens up, in **patterns** here and there;
A mix of **GAS** and **LIQUIDS** shoots up into the **AIR**!
Volcanic vents are chimneys with much **ENERGY** to spare;
They free **hot emanations** from **MAGMA's chambered upper layer.**

Steam and **water** settle, first filling the **deepest crustal bends**;
Then overflow and coalesce till **water's** reach extends
To limits of **THE ONE OCEAN** between the **mountain trends**
THE ONE OCEAN and **THE ONE LAND** really are **good friends**!

That's how **THE ONE OCEAN** came to
be, and also **THE ONE AIR**…
From the **liquids** and the **gases** that came from **way down there.**
THE ONE OCEAN and **THE ONE LAND**
MASS, make quite a **balanced** pair,
But **mountain building processes** give **living things** a scare!

The **LAND** above the **OCEAN** falls victim to **erosion**;
Airborne ocean water blows landward; **its rains cause corrosion**!
Weather weakens the **rock**; **gravity** returns it
and water to **THE ONE OCEAN**,
Where **sediments** and **chemicals** form **nutritious life-force potion,**

For **algal growth, plankton, nekton** and higher **living forms**
Dwelling within **THE ONE OCEAN** and **surviving** hostile storms,
To **pass genetic codes** along **to growing brand new swarms**
Of marine, terrestrial and aerial **LIFE** to reach their present quorums!

SIMPLY, THAT'S THE STORY!

The above poem was written by Donald W.C. Harris Mar. 3, 2010;
a simple summary of several billions of years of Earth's history.

THE WORLD COULD
USE OUR HELP!

The world could use our help right ***now*** to put us all at ease...
Some jolly jokes and fun-filled stuff...p'rhaps pepper to make us sneeze!

Bolts of humour travel far when trying to appease
In times of stress and deep duress when press begins to squeeze!

Lighten up; make us laugh; send love on wings of angels' breeze.
Behold all earth's blessings...fertile gardens and all trees!

Appreciate clean waters, ice and all the seas.
Remember, all's connected to flowers, birds and bees.

No-one wants pollution...it's like a bad disease!
And no-one needs to hunger...or be so cold they freeze!

So let's all tend to matters, ***now*** down on bended knees;
Begin to make improvements; I beg ***you***, won't you please?

Written for all humanity and life forms
by Donald W. C. Harris, October 18th, 2007.

WHITE ROCKS AND RED ROSES

With white rocks and red roses, our garden we started;
We both had dreams but too much baggage we carted.
Over the years we took sole paths yet uncharted,
Rarely together, we thought it best if we parted!

With more rocks than roses, our garden of weeds,
No longer attends to our dreams and our needs,
It's so overrun by just thorns without seeds,
'Cause our love we once had got spoiled by bad deeds!

Our love for each other dwindled slowly away…
The natural result of our own separate, selfish way!
Now more rocks than roses have taken full sway,
And the white rocks and weeds mock our disarray!

Do we have a chance to plant our garden anew?
Can we tend it carefully, rocks and red roses too?
Can we garden together, be fair and be true,
Like partners in projects are rightly meant to!

Maybe we'd start out with one family pet,
To see how it goes before kids we get!
If we play together and don't have to fret,
A family of children would be a sure bet!

Starting with one child, and then maybe two,
Then on and on 'til we had quite a few,
Along with our pets in our home-grown zoo,
We'd care for all and each other with love true!

IT'S ABOUT WE, NOT JUST ME!

The above poem was written by Donald W. C. Harris 2010-08-10.

ONENESS/
LEADERSHIP

A FEW RECORD-SETTING OLYMPIANS

Eight plus seven medals: that adds up to fifteen.
Eight gold records, seven worlds; that is mighty keen!
Fastest in the water...that's **Michael Phelps**' dream.
What really counts for history is: he did it all so clean!

Running star, **Usain Bolt** ("**Lightning**" that is),
Is fastest on the ground, where he truly means biz!
At six foot five inches tall, **Usain** is just all fizz!
Nine point six nine seconds! This record is all his!

Canada's **Eric Lamaze**, is amazing!
Clearing all jumps on "**Hickstead**" with no fazing!
First solitary gold; this team's surely blazing
Trails to a world of **ONENESS**...by **love**, not by hazing!

Emilie Heymans is a diver supreme,
A fit young lady who's fulfilling her dream.
Her silver medal win (nearly gold) soothes like cream;
Puts a smile on her face that sun rays can't out beam!

Ten-pin bowler **Jason Walker**, of Brampton, I've been told,
Has won many medals in **Special Olympics** balls rolled.
His notable achievements, almost match his heart of gold,
And inspire other hopefuls as their precious lives unfold!

There are so many **others** who deserve some space right here,
For **everyone**, on this earth, is worthy; that's so clear!
Praise brings **glory** and **peace** to **ONE**! **No one** needs a smear!
This approach helps **humankind** advance from year to year.

WHATEVER YOU DO...DO RIGHT!

Written by Donald W.C. Harris October 28th,
2008, to inspire acceptance of diversity.

ACT FOR ONE!

You and I, are us and we...
ALL are ONE; ever will be!
These and those, them and they...
ALL together, do ONE's way!

With cracks sealed, none fall through!
They can't...if ONE can count on you!
If each person does right things, too...
That's when ONENESS will come true!

Don't shy away from doing right;
You'll sleep calmly every night,
And never feel a fear or fright.
Clean our world, now, site by site!

It just takes one to make a start...
Soon, all persons do their part!
Things get better, like a speeding dart.
Do you agree...that's ONENESS smart?

Let's ALL pitch in; get this job done!
Let's make life good for everyone...
For each mom, daughter, dad and son!
THE SOURCE is pleased! ALL act for ONE!

ACT FOR THE GOOD
OF ALL...FOR ONENESS!

The above poem was written to better all that is,
by Donald W. C. Harris, August 2nd, 2009.

ALL RIGHT DOUGH

Once you've become **ONE**,
You've become everyone!
More **good things** get done,
And **life** takes on more **fun**!

Once you've arrived there,
You've been everywhere!
You've learned how to **care,**
And discovered how to **share**!

When you've won your wings,
You can do many things!
Hear how your **heart sings**!
Shed all your mood swings!

Once you've climbed above cloud,
It means you're not too proud
To practice **virtues** out loud,
And **fulfill** the **acts** you **vowed**!

You've found the **good inside,**
Now there's nothing left to hide!
Open chakras really wide!
Let **Spirit** be your **guide**!

Once you've **let** the **ego go,**
You'll find **all will flow**!
Knead only all right dough,
To let your **ONENESS** show!

HEARTS SING, IF YOU
DO THE RIGHT THING!

The above poem was written by Donald W. C. Harris 2010-09-19.
It was written for everyone, everywhere, to better human interaction.

ALL...ONENESS LEGENDS!

Please swallow my seed;
It's all you will need!
Just take the lead,
And absorb all my mead!

You have me in your creed;
I am you when you bleed!
ALL are **ONE**...let's concede,
No matter the breed!

ALL are **KINSFOLK**...
Of the same yolk;
Let's go for broke,
As this is no joke!

Blow away smoke,
Before **WE ALL** croak!
In full **ONENESS** soak...
WE're **ALL** the same spoke!

Let's **ALL** be best friends;
Make **OUR** total amends,
So hostility ends
And egoism just bends!

So **EVERYONE** blends,
And overextends...
To be **LOVE** that mends!
ALL...**ONENESS LEGENDS**!

MAKE ONENESS LEGENDARY!

Written for **ALL** of **US** everywhere, forever,
by Donald W. C. Harris, April 12th, 2009.

ARE YOU AWARE?

Are you aware of **ONENESS** yet?
A great safe haven, so place your bet!
Point your compass; make sure it's set.
Meet with **ONENESS**...you won't regret.

People in darkness, stumble and fall;
That won't happen when you're with **ALL!**
ONENESS folk find light...stand tall.
This **ONENESS** program, now install!

Don't stop and think...just open up;
Embrace the light and fill your cup.
Marry **ONENESS** without *pre-nup*!
Awesome feeling! You've wakened up!

No more reason for being greedy;
You'll find your peace in helping needy.
Good thoughts and deeds uplift the seedy.
ONENESS guards the weak and geeky.

Choose right now to spread the word...
That **ONE** is each; that's not absurd.
Let go your crap, in one huge turd!
You will soar like a fledgling bird.

YOU'RE NOW FLYING...RIGHT?

Written for each and every one of us and all life
by Donald W. C. Harris, August 4th, 2008.

BECOMING COLOUR BLIND

I'm black...but what's that spot I see?
That white spot, yes, is part of me.
Perhaps, it's there symbolically?
To help me set all persons free!

That one white blotch (soon there were three)...
In time, the white, stood out on me.
At first, I hid in shame, you see...
With matching make-up, I tried to flee.

With white skin patches over much of me,
My cover-up efforts were futility...
Then, I knew spots were meant to be,
And their acceptance my reality.

Black and white is not that clear;
Thoughts of difference can incite fear;
But **ONENESS** invites **ALL** near!
Knowing this, I don't feel that queer.

Hurrah for **ONENESS**! It's the only way...
To rid the world of hate and fray;
To squelch ideas for conquering prey...
Please think **ONENESS** every day.

TUNE INTO ONENESS WORLD!

Written for all life for all time by Donald W. C. Harris, July 31st, 2008.

BEING IS...

BEING is...to be
Entirely free...
To see **you** as **me**!
How can that be?

Despite different sizes,
And other disguises...
When one realizes,
ONENESS resides us!

UNIVERSE is **ALL**...
Vibes...big and small...
In mountain peaks tall;
In **LIFE**'s growth...and fall!

Nothing is separate...
Whether famed or desperate;
Schooled or illiterate...
Just a rock or a wavelet!

Everything, everyone...
All together...tightly strung!
On one strand, **ALL** is hung!
That's how **ONENESS'** song is sung!

VIBRATE IN TUNE
WITH ONENESS!

Written for **ALL**...persons, processes and things...for the sake of
ONENESS, by Donald W. C. Harris, May 29th, 2009.

CANADA'S NEW GOLDEN 'CAN-DO' OF 2010

Canada's team harvested gold
Medals galore! They'll not be sold!
Personal 'bests' fulfilled the fold!
Weather was sun, snow, rain and cold.

Team spirit was high…high as the sky;
That was the key, and here is why:
Spirit's the force, the power which by,
Undying ONENESS opens third eye!

Canada's team showed what could be done,
With ethics and efforts along with some fun;
All joined in the goal to be part of the ONE,
Then oozed skills and wills to reach for the sun!

Focus with me on what true teamwork means:
It's working together that captures best scenes,
For old folks, young folks, and even the teens,
And also for babies in pink or blue jeans;
(Include all the genomes and all of the genes!)

Teamwork means no one toils all alone
To strive to bring a gold medal home.
Someone is needed to keep muscle tone,
And soothe away soreness, when pain causes groan!

The point, now, is this, my healing friends:
Nothing's really over until it ends!
Right now, I think Canada, this message sends:
The world needs ONENESS to help make amends!

U CAN-DO 2!

Donald W.C. Harris wrote this poem Feb. 28th, 2010 as tribute
to the limitless potential of human spirit that calls for peace.

CHOOSE A LIFE

Are you the **one** who leads **life** as a doer?
Or among the throng feeling scorched on a skewer?
Or one of the many in hordes in a sewer?
Or maybe you spend time steeped in manure?

If **you** are in need of a **life** more fulfilling,
Just decide it...and do it! Step away from the grilling!
Better **your life** by becoming more willing...
Look forward to reaching your ecstasy trilling!

By offering first, **your help** where there's need...
Yes, **you** may start a chain-reaction, indeed!
For often, first action is merely a **seed**...
That **germinates** more **aid**, once **you**'ve set the lead!

Everything's possible...**you** will soon learn;
Myths to the contrary...soon will all burn.
Right things from wrong...we all must discern...
To progress to **ONENESS**...all wrong we must spurn!

Cooperation's key to **ONE**'s **paradise** and **love**,
For **ALL** to enjoy, as in **heaven** above,
Where **ALL** are cozy, as warm hand in wool glove...
Where **ALL** can sing freely, like **PEACE loving dove**!

WE ALL need to learn that we won't really win...
Until **WE** know **WE**'re **ALL ONE** for the sake of **ALL kin**,
No matter **OUR** birthplace...or **colour** of skin...
The fact **WE**'re **ALL human**...can never be sin!

MAKE YOUR MOVE TO ONENESS!

Written for all humanity, by Donald W. C.
Harris, December 28th, 2008.

COUNTRIES WITHOUT BORDERS

Countries without borders merge with all the rest;
That way there's only **ONE!** Of course, it is the best.
LOVE for **every person** would be **our** biggest test;
Embracing **one another** is right, **I** would suggest!

Once **we**'ve held **each other** and shown that **we** care,
OUR WORLD would be like heaven...**ONENESS** would be there.
Every heart and **soul,** would be included in **our prayer**;
Around each dinner table, there'd be no missing chair!

No one would feel separate, or left out of **OUR** fold;
And age would not matter...from young to very old...
Not **one** would be forgotten, to gather dust and mould.
And not a single **person,** would then be bought or sold!

With **everyone** included, and all dignity preserved,
ALL would be contributing...**ONENESS** would be served.
No matter what **OUR** challenges, **we**'d face them all unnerved...
And find **just right** answers, for every pitch that's curved!

We would have real **power** to better **every life**...
To rid the pain and suffering that causes so much strife...
That plague this **WORLD** with problems, so ugly and so rife...
That wound **HUMANITY** to its **bone**...deep cuts with jagged knife!

Rewards of numbing borders of every country soon,
Would be **WORLD**'s team of **ONENESS**, playing **ALL** in tune...
From dawn to dusk in sunshine...from rise to fall of moon...
ALL's **ONENESS WORLD** a symphony...tranquil...as a loon!

LET'S ALL GET IT...TOGETHER!

Written for the betterment of **ALL HUMANITY**,
by Donald W. C. Harris, March 15th, 2009.

DO FORGIVE

Some things remembered would be better left forgotten…
Ugly things, like memories of moments that were rotten!
Unless a memory's pleasant, like warm, fuzzy balls of cotton,
It's best to let it go! Now that suggestion's really spot-on!

To relive the negatives is pointless; can't you see?
For it's **living every moment** that really lets **one be**
The **person God intended**! Doing **right** keeps **one free**
To **help Him** build our **ONENESS** for **humanity**'s **liberty**!

You can be a vital spoke to better someone's day.
When all are in the wheel of **love**, things roll **ONENESS**' way,
Wherein there are no putdowns or bullying of prey,
Instead, a world of sunshine without those clouds of grey!

Humanity needs each of us to stand up for what's **right**,
For only then, world evils will be vanquished from our sight.
And only then, all people will focus on **God**'s **white light**
To have **eternal peace** within, without the need to fight!

Nothing is as wonderful as knowing **inner beauty**,
And hearing inner **harmonies** without war calls to duty!
God's **treasures** are around us; **His natural laws** are booty!
Each person wears a **happy face**; that makes each one a cutie!

So only **live** the **moment** for the **best life** has to give;
If someone does you wrong, then be sure you **do forgive**!
You're ready now for the **next instant** in the **life** you're meant to **live**!
Choose **ONENESS** as your model where **love** is **life**'s best sieve!

FORGIVE! THEN LIVE!

The above poem was written by Donald W. C. Harris 2010-11-20.

DO YOU FEEL GOOD...?

Do **YOU** feel good about all **YOU**'ve done?
Have **YOU** ever wronged or harmed **SOMEONE**?
Then make amends; lifelong friends become!
Ask for forgiveness! Know **WE ALL** are **ONE**!

Narrow pride's a problem...it never is the answer...
Unless it accommodates each and every dancer.
Ego spreads exclusion, like a fast growing cancer;
It counters **ALL OUR ONENESS**, like jabs from a lancer!

Survival of the fittest does not really apply
To **human** evolution...and here's the reason why;
ALL are **SPIRITUAL BEINGS**, with **ONE** compassionate dye!
OUR overwhelming **ONENESS** is **OUR** key and common tie!

Overcoming urges to undermine another,
Demands **OUR** conscious vigil and care for every **BROTHER**;
OUR EARTH is for **EVERYONE**; **SHE**
is **OUR** nurturing **MOTHER**!
Be fair and kind to **ALL**...never helping **ONE** to smother!

Be **ONE** with **GOD**...**OUR** steadfast common rudder!
HUMANITY will be better, like **BABES** with precious udder,
If **ALL** of **US** respect **ALL LIFE**, and never make **IT** shudder;
HUMANKIND will **ALL** have **PEACE**! No evil words **WE**'ll mutter!

ONENESS IS GOOD FOR ALL!

Written for **ALL** by Donald W. C. Harris, May 18th,
2009. (Note: verse five was completed, May 18th, 2009;
all others were written two to three months earlier.)

EGO SNARE

That was then...this is now.
How time flies! I wonder...how?
What has happened to the Dow?
Value hugs the paths of Tao!

No matter how the markets go...
Up, or down, or to and fro,
We're **ALL** together **sis** and **bro**!
We're **ONE**! **You** and **I, we** know!

ALL must succeed...or **ALL** will fail!
If not for **ONE**...it's garbage pail!
Some can't be plump while **others** frail!
ALL must be on **OUR ONENESS** trail!

Each must practice fair and square,
Or end up in the ego snare...
Lonely, wretched, feeling bare...
And worried that no one will ever care!

If **each person** does no harm,
Instills no fear...sparks no alarm,
ALL find fun, peace, joy and charm!
Welcome **ALL**...to **ONENESS'** farm!

TAKE CARE OF BIZ...
MAKE ONENESS FIZZ!

Written for the progress of **ALL PERSONS** everywhere,
by Donald W. C. Harris, August 25-27th, 2009.

EGO'S PRIDE

Nobody really understands anyone.
Traditions slow change from getting 'right' done.
Some beliefs hold us back and should come undone.
Does ego's pride keep you from **ONE**?

Everything everywhere under the sun,
Is really united…on one string it's strung.
To think separation, is like breath without lung.
Gasping and wheezing, **ONE**'s song can't get sung!

Energy vibration is the common tie
That binds all to **ONE,** and that is why
A wee puff of gas affects all birds that fly,
And human behaviour reacts to the sky.

Not one thing escapes the **SOURCE** of vibration;
The death of one child impacts all creation.
A few drops of water can enhance conversation,
Political speech and a poet's oration.

All affects all, no matter the station!

Do not let traditions block your right view.
Open your window! Let the sunshine through!
Accommodate! That's the right thing to do.
Get into **ONENESS**! It welcomes you!

THE RIGHT SHIP…
FRIENDSHIP!

The above poem was written by Donald W. C. Harris 2010-04-25.
It was written for everyone and everything, everywhere.

ETHICS HIGH...

Go to cash...before the crash;
Then celebrate with your stash,
By spending when the price is slashed.
That's how hopes will not be dashed!

Go to gold...when guvs get bold...
And overheap the bills you fold;
When economies turn ice cold,
Lock in wealth with treasures gold!

When jobs get rare and people scared,
Be creative! Take on that dare!
Be unafraid! Avoid despair!
Be truly you, no matter where!

Go forward with your ethics high;
Tell whole truths, and never lie!
Bravely stretch to touch the sky,
Where hopes and dreams cannot die!

Be kind to others; treat them fair...
And know that **ONE** is always there!
GOD knows truth...exposed, we're bare!
Do right things! Pay fair share! Really care!

A better world...is all we ask
For **ALL** of **US**...**WE** face the task,
Of just plain living without a mask!
Let's drink together from **ONENESS'** flask!

LOVE; BE LOVED;
FEAR NOUGHT!

Written by Donald W. C. Harris, October 8th, 2009 with
hope that **ALL** of **US** everywhere progress together in
peace until we attain universal and eternal **PEACE**.

EVERYONE IS SPECIAL

Everyone is special! That really is my point.
All of us are queens and kings that, **yes**, we must anoint.
Loving care with respect always helps improve the joint...
And makes each heart and spirit soul feel extremely buoyant.

Everyone is special!...Of that one can be sure.
There's not a single being whose heart cannot be pure.
Though some go astray 'cause of trials that they endure,
Our **inclusive understanding** can bring about their cure.

Exclusion is out! **Inclusion,** no doubt...
Is the **secret substance** for solving world gout.
Contribution by all makes the **all** strong and stout.
Co-operation devout--this process will bring us about.

Let all this world's nations forget about borders...
Expand beyond notions of have-nots and hoarders.
Hearts, spirits and souls can be cures for disorders.
Mother Nature provides **all**...Come then, let's escort **Her**!

Written for all, December 9th, 2006, by Donald W. C. Harris in the
belief of justice and fairness in the harmonious world to come soon.

FLOW-THROUGH THOUGHTS

My flow-through **thoughts** hit **ALL** right spots;
They stop **ALL** clots and tied up knots,
And keep **me free** from all onslaughts!
My head stays **open**...that counts lots!

I'm always ready for **inspiration**;
When **it** comes, **it**'s like dictation.
The messages are for **every nation**,
What does not matter? **My** location.

Thoughts of **goodness**, meant for **ALL**,
Flow freely from the **SOURCE**...no stall!
They're bound to build **ONE**'s confidence wall
So long...and strong...it cannot fall!

Knowing **WE** are **ALL** protected,
And that **WE ALL** have been selected,
None of **US** can be infected...
Or ever be misdirected.

For **every path** that **WE** may choose,
Provides **white light** with **all right** clues.
Everyone has paid **ONE**'s dues!
ALL are ready...so fire the fuse!

Off **WE** fly upon ignition!
OUR ONENESS trip comes to fruition,
Uniting ALL with **ONE's** ambition...
To **better ALL HUMAN condition**!

GET FIRED UP
ABOUT ONENESS!

Written for **better relationships** among and between **all peoples**,
by Donald W. C. Harris, June 22nd, 2009.

FORGETTING TO REMEMBER

Forgetting to remember sounds much like a disease,
But when it comes to grudges, to forget puts minds at ease!
Is there any use in holding **thoughts** that cannot ever please?
Forgive! Then let them go, or they'll keep you in deep freeze!

Paralyzed, you can't progress beyond your state of ill;
Let evil thoughts escape from you and never wish ill will!
You'll never move ahead in **life** while contemplating "kill".
Fuel yourself with **wholesome things**; be sure to get your fill!

By doing that, it won't be long before you're making strides
To **help** yourself and others feel better from insides.
Important things start getting done with fewer backward slides,
And **Spirits** now can enter; they want to be your guides!

Help's out there for everyone; the **Universe** is rich!
Allow yourself to tap it; just turn on the **right** switch!
Good things can come to those who cling to **ONENESS**' noble hitch!
Start **living righteously, right** now; avoid **life**'s dirty ditch!

You'll improve the way you **feel** and how you look at **life**,
When you start **helping others**, you'll start ridding self of strife!
Every child, each person, and every man and wife
Need you to be a player, for them to hear your fife!

Forgetting to remember? Is that a **blessing in disguise**?
Some may find this message **hopeful,** even wise;
Know nothing can be gained if we keep on telling lies!
Be principled in the way you **live**! ONENESS has best buys!

FORGIVE! THEN FORGET!
ISN'T THAT ONE'S BEST BET?

The above poem was written by Donald W. C. Harris 2010-09-22.
It was written for the **benefit** of **ALL**.

GET CAUGHT BY ONENESS' PLOT!

ME is WE means YOU are I;
On that truth, ONE can rely.
That WE are ALL, ONE can't deny...
Knowing this, YOU're set to fly!

In your spaceship feeling high,
Meet with ANGELS in the sky.
YOU may know some passersby...
But never know the reasons why!

It's not important if YOU do not...
The magic is...YOU have your spot,
Like ALL the OTHERS not forgot;
YOU ALL are part of UNIVERSE' pot!

No SOUL escapes; WE ALL get caught
By ONENESS' plot! WE're freed...not fraught
With greed and guns that cost a lot...
And doom ALL bodies to pointless slot!

SOULS and SPIRITS will endure!
Bodies decay, just like manure!
ENERGY transformation is for sure!
Body fascination...a useless tour!

SPIRIT EVOLUTION
IS ONENESS CURE!

Written for EVERYONE in the SPIRIT of ONENESS,
By Donald W. C. Harris, June 1st, 2009.

HEAR TODAY...OUR ONENESS ONLY!

Hear today...gone tomorrow;
Each day after...filled with sorrow!
Quake disaster...it's no *el* toro!
There's never any time to borrow!

Aftershocks are sure to come;
Walls of buildings...gone off plumb!
Think it's over? Really *dumb*!
Noise? It's deafening, like a drum!

Debris is almost everywhere.
People's faces all show scare!
Shelves, if standing...almost bare!
Yes, **life** for many, seems unfair!

Why must **lives** face such test?
Is it to save only the best?
If so, what happens to **all** the rest?
Those that cross, are they not blessed?

Know **each person** is also **other**...
ALL together, **sis** and **brother**;
Therefore **ONE**, hence **ALL** are **mother**!
ALL GOD's **children** cannot smother!

So...on and on and on **WE** try.
OUR many earthly roles belie
The **TRUTH** of **ONENESS**! Let **US** rely
On **ONENESS** only! Hear its cry!

ONE'S PURPOSE...PEACE!

Written for **PEACE** for **ALL,** everywhere,
by Donald W. C. Harris, October 3rd, 2009.

KNOW WHY YOU ARE HERE

Know why you are here?
Is your purpose clear?
When no one is near,
Have you feelings of fear?

Embrace the moments you have all alone;
They give you a chance to assess how you've grown;
To recall all results of the seeds you have sown.
Could you feel safe if your deeds were all known?

Whatever it is that you've done in the past,
Only the good things are things that will last...
For good always wins and evil's outcast.
From now on be sure to behave unsurpassed.

Your purpose, now known, as part of the whole,
Is to help out others, thus, enrich **ONE**'s soul.
As you broaden **ONENESS** and fill up **ONE**'s bowl,
You've wakened awareness to your **ONE** major goal.

And the happy ending to the **ONENESS** story...
When each has entered its bowl of glory...
There won't be a place for scenes that are gory,
Like ends of worlds, or Sodom and Gomorrah.

DO YOUR PART...ENTER
THE BOWL OF ONENESS!

Written by Donald W. C. Harris, August 3rd, 2008 from inside the bowl
for a wholesome universe. Please choose to join me right now.

LIFE BEYOND

Life beyond our planet...is there?
Are **we** all exposed? Naked; bare!
Whence have **we** come...what lair?
Journey forward? Cautious; take care!

Enough damage done? Surely yes!
Move slowly now...cure **our** mess!
Most of **us** guilty? Let **us** confess!
Act together for **ALL**'s good...success!

Fairness for few? Not good enough!
Each is important! That's right stuff!
Shedding bad baggage and ridding of fluff
Will power **all persons** to **love** with no guff!

Do **good** for **one**! That's good for **ALL**!
That means **no one** is dropping the ball.
With **no one** too big and **no one** too small,
Everyone's covered! **No one** will fall!

With all of the greed and selfishness gone...
And **persons** all over not feeling withdrawn,
Spirits uplift to the **heavens** beyond...
Such is the scene as **our ONENESS** moves on!

UPLIFT ALL AROUND YOU!

Written for **ALL** everywhere, by Donald W.
C. Harris, August 14-15, 2009.

MAP-LINES

We're all in a gang; believe that or not!
Each nation, by boundaries, defines its own spot.
But national pride slows **ONE**'s blood to clot…
Unless all the people have been **ONENESS** taught!

Borders and boundaries are blocks to the flow
Of cross-border friendships and good(nes)s on the go.
Political outlines are not natural, you know;
They stem from greed, and strike **ONENESS** a blow!

No other life forms accept man-made map-lines.
Only we humans must read all of the signs,
And if we fail here…we all pay the fines!
We set our own traps, and all the land mines!

Until we see each **person** as part of all others,
And **value their being** as **ONE of our brothers**,
Include them as **family**; treat them kindly like **mothers**…
ONENESS will struggle while progress just smothers!

Take a fresh look at the **life** you are leading;
If you're holding grudges and prolonging bleeding,
Turn a new leaf! Watch out what you're seeding!
Send love and hugs every chance, every greeting!

ONENESS will reign! It only takes time…
The shorter the better, so let's **all shed the slime**.
Start acting with **wisdom** of **ONENESS** sublime!
Practise just loving! Make ONENESS prime!

MAKE MAP-LINES MEANINGLESS!

The above poem was written by Donald W. C.
Harris March 02, 2010, as a prayer
for perfect human relationships around the
world and **for world peace, forever**!

NO ONE EXCLUSIVE

Every someone is partly me!
No one exclusive can ever be!
This view of life is easy to see;
Showing kindness to all is good for *we.*

Each in this world needs to know love...
Instead of the torment of rude push and shove.
There's love from **ONE** other that fits like a glove...
It comes from the *source* on high, up above.

Know that you have it while you are here,
That with it for comfort, there's no need to fear
Ever being alone without friend or dear.
All this I express with feelings sincere.

Do your part to raise common vibration;
Join in the instrument of **ONE** excitation!
Good energy flow needs much channel dilation
To eliminate blocks and gross devastation.

There's really no need for earthly disaster;
Realize now, we all have the **ONE MASTER!**
Giver of all...to all is not alabaster...
Believe in this sooner, for success all the faster!

Somewhere in space, Earth's been given the grace...
An elegant lace, to better its place...
By hosting some beings of our human race.
Intelligent beings: "Let's embrace...not disgrace"!

Written by Donald W. C. Harris, February 24th, 2008, with hope
for enlightenment for everyone as we take a giant stride forward.

ON REACHING ONE HUNDRED

On reaching one hundred years on this Earth,
You've had much to challenge your state of mirth.
It's been a long time from your date of birth...
Powerful emotions have streamed to your firth!

You've witnessed history repeat many wrongs;
Humankind has harmed many throngs...
Too many persons sang not their true songs,
And stifled WORLD ONENESS, to which ALL belongs!

But ONES who live long, earn protection, I guess,
And fear is a stranger they safely transgress...
Over and over, with no needs to confess,
Their souls carry forward, in spite of duress!

Just being themselves, they show us success,
And help rid the world from all of its mess...
Making ONE more...not making ONE less!
Know ALL the worlds' peoples, ONE GOD does bless!

YOU ARE ONE OF ONENESS!
HAPPY ONE HUNDREDTH BIRTHDAY!

Written for friend Eileen's 100th birthday celebration,
by Donald W. C. Harris, January 24th, 2009.

ONENESS CAN POWER
HUMANITY'S TIDE

"Made-off" and *"Stand-for"*...of evil ilk,
Care naught for their victims and souls they bilk.
Thieves like them, are as slippery as silk;
Their greed does harm...like poison in milk!

Ill gotten riches always make matters worse;
Even the stealers of the stolen purse,
Are haunted constantly, by nightmarish curse;
Those who've been robbed...their wealth's dispersed!

The greed of the few changes harmony to noise...
Depriving the many from cause to rejoice,
And widening the gap, and depleting the toys...
Squelching opportunities for girls and for boys!

If you've been like *"Made-off"* or *"Stand-for"* or such,
Now's a good chance to revamp your touch.
You're not too late to help those on a crutch.
You can do better by giving back much!

Your positive efforts to be just and kind,
Will improve the world and bring peace of mind,
Not just to you, but even the blind...
Who will "see" your effects...humanity refined!

Your noble actions will spawn far and wide,
The spirit of **ONENESS, ALL** need inside,
Deep in our hearts, where right thoughts reside.
ONENESS can power humanity's tide!
ONENESS can harness humanity's pride!

BE BETTER...FOR ALL!

Written for **ALL** everywhere in the **UNIVERSE,**
by Donald W. C. Harris, February 24th, 2009.

ONENESS LOOM

From mother's womb to cold stone tomb,
LIVES are cast in **EARTH**'s living room.
WE weave **OUR LIVES** on the **ONENESS** loom...
And use resources **WE ALL** consume.

Together, **WE** will fully bloom,
As **ONE** flows in **OUR** inclusive flume...
Always clear of impending doom;
WE're **ALL** kept clean by the **ONENESS** broom.

There is no room for sadness and gloom,
So feel just joy of bride and groom.
No depression remains to assume,
For righteous paths lead to heaven! Zoom!

ONENESS is the new age buzz...
Results? Only good that's soft as fuzz!
ONENESS' spirit knows that's because...
ONENESS works! It really does!

No one wants to be a leech;
Teachers...practise what you preach!
And politicians, we beseech,
Help **ALL of US** enjoy **ONE's** beach!

HOPE TO SEE YOU ALL
IN HEAVEN SOME DAY!

Written for everyone, by Donald W. C. Harris, July 30th, 2008.

ONENESS QUIRK

Isn't it time, society
Resurrected integrity,
Honesty, trust and dignity…
Best attributes of humanity?

What happened to sensitivity,
Compassion, feeling lovingly,
Sharing welfare unsparingly…
Doing all these willingly?

We've been careless with fairness,
And lost our awareness
Of the force of a caress.
Yes, we've made quite a mess!

But all is not lost;
At very small cost,
All bad can be tossed,
And just good embossed!

Here's what to do.
Think and act new…
Do for all, not few!
Become a new you!

Quit being a jerk!
And no longer shirk;
Dedicate good work,
To our **ONENESS QUIRK**!

DO YOUR BIT;
HELP RID SHIT!

Written by Donald W. C. Harris, December 20th, 2009,
for the **best** of **Humanity** for **all persons**, everywhere.

ONENESS' WHEEL

Forgive yourself; build self esteem!
Then **progress**, and **live** your **dream**,
With **all others** in **GOD**'s **grand scheme**
To have **us all** on **ONENESS' team**!

A **perfect world** would be **ideal**;
What's needed is for **all** to **feel**
Respected, loved, and get **fair deal**;
Kindness drives ONENESS' wheel!

Helping others brings **peace of mind**;
There's nothing more to being kind,
Than being there…not being blind.
Befriend ALL, with ties that bind!

By giving help, your message is clear.
You let them know that you are near;
And **they can go on…in love**, not fear,
Forever **grateful**, to **you, my dear**!

Know that **you mean much to ONE**!
(That feels so good, you crave **more fun**);
Spread your love beyond Earth's **sun**…
You'll have your **taste** of **ONENESS' bun**!

BE KIND, NOT BLIND!

The above poem was written by Donald W. C. Harris,
March 1st (verses 1, 2 and 3), and March 4th (verses 4 and 5), 2010.

ONENESS...HEAR ITS CALL!

Live balanced ecstasy;
Float as in isostasy;
Be free in ultra-harmony...
State of bliss that **ALL** can be!

Heads at peace...
Not tense; feel release!
Caressed in fleece...
SPIRIT flows increase!

Problems are nought;
Have we forgot?
There is no knot,
Can undo thought!

Let come what may...
At end of day,
ONENESS has full sway...
Everything is okay!

With **PEACE** for **ALL**,
Ascend...and never fall!
Erect...and always tall!
ONENESS...Hear **its** call!

Each of us can do it;
Determine...and pursue it!
Now done, you always knew it;
You're **ONE**! Get right into it!

BE ONE!

Written for ALL everywhere, by Donald W. C. Harris, May 20th, 2009.

ONE'S CONTRACT

Please drink of **me**, while **I** drink of **you**!
Our juices unite us, making one of two.
Our holes we open for **each** to view;
In turn, **we** fill them with **our glue**!

Together, we're as **all** need be,
Wholly **blessed** and feeling **free**,
In arms of **love**, endlessly
Safe from harm, in revelry!

All persons must realize
That **WE**'re **ALL ONE**, in **GOD**'s eyes;
HE sees **WE ALL** wear just **ONE** size,
And **ALL TOGETHER** win **HIS prize**!

When **ALL** appreciate this fact,
There'll be no holding **ONENESS** back,
As **ONENESS** will remain intact,
Uniting **ALL**, by **ALL**'s **ONE CONTRACT**!

Forever joined and **purpose bent**,
And needing only **ONE**'s consent,
Not even **ONE** will dare resent
That **ONENESS** holds **OUR BEST CONTENT**!

BRING ON OUR BEST;
GO FOR ONENESS!

The above poem was written by Donald W.
C. Harris, February 19th, 2010,
for all to become Humanity's best beings.

ONLY ONENESS

Me is **we** in **everything**;
I touch **all** when **I** crawl and cling.
My voice is in all birds that sing;
I fly with them on every wing.

Not one action escapes another;
I hurt the world if **I** harm a **brother**.
Even trees, my thoughts can smother.
Earth needs **me**! **I** am her **mother**!

All things and **life** have **fields** entwined;
These threads of **energy** grip and bind;
Not one **vibration** gets left behind!
The **POWER** of **ONENESS** boggles the mind!

Every **particle, wave** and **thought,**
Is bound in one forget-me-(k)not!
A grand lasso holds every spot...
Only **ONENESS**...that's **ALL** we've got!

Consider all difference for all it's worth;
Careful inclusion can start rebirth;
Reuniting should spark joy and mirth.
Together, **NOW**! Let's broaden **our** girth!

ONENESS AWARENESS!
IT'S WONDERFUL! JOIN
ME ON THE JOURNEY.

Written by Donald W. C. Harris, April 7th, 2008 to benefit everyone and everything everywhere in the UNIVERSE.

PARTS OF THE POOL

We are all parts of the pool of **life**!
Swimmers, floaters and sinkers have strife…
All brothers and sisters, each husband and wife!
Though each seems distinct, our **sameness is rife**!

Every one and every thing endeavours to grow;
Even the "lifeless"…more than we know!
Everything vibrates, up, down, to and fro!
If this is not true, then I'll have to eat crow!

Energy flows from its **vibration source**;
It knows where to travel to keep on its course,
Affecting surroundings, whether mass or just pores,
Including all persons, from babies to whores!

No thing and no one are truly separate!
We all are each other; that's a safe bet!
So don't harm a thing, for you might regret
Whatever it is you flush down a toilet!

Love and **be kind** to all around you;
Respect environment and all persons too!
The time to **right wrong** is long past due!
We've all made mistakes, in fact, quite a few!

Forgive and let go of all of the crap;
Be loving and **thoughtful**; put down the strap!
We're all **ONE** child in **GOD**'s spirit lap!
Isn't it time for **GOD**'s **ONENESS** map?

ONE IS ALL!

The above poem was written by Donald W. C. Harris 2010-07-11.
It was written for the wholeness of the
universe and for peace throughout.

PUERTO RICAN LADY

Puerto Rican **lady, you** are truly a **treasure**;
You're **worthy** and **dignified** by every measure.
Getting to know **you** is an ultimate pleasure!
Your partner is **blessed** to have **you** at his leisure!

You're **honest** and **forthright** and so **full** of **love**...
Your every move comes from **heaven** above!
You're duty bound to **embrace**, not to shove;
Your **love** flies on **wings** of every **peace dove**!

The **world** needs **ALL persons** to be much like **you**...
Thoughtful, bold, daring and **delightful** too!
Your light lifts up **spirits** when they may be blue.
You're **willing** to drive, or be passenger **true**!

You're **smart**, have **wisdom** and **feelings** intense;
Inside **your** body, rests a **spirit immense**.
Your soul's **experience** is **full** of much **sense**!
Hearts make the **homes**...not material contents!

You aim to **protect all** that's **right** from the wrongs.
ONENESS needs **you** to **sing** loudly its songs
To help reach the masses, the gangs and the throngs.
HOPE is in **ONENESS**! **ONENESS** belongs!

Until **every person** feels **included** by **ALL**,
And **each loves oneself**, the **short** and the **tall**,
The **sick** and the **poor**, the **weak** ones who fall,
No one is **anyone**...and **ONENESS** will stall!

HOPE LIVES...IN
ONENESS' HOME!

Written for ALL people everywhere (but
dedicated to a new-found friend
who knows who she is), by Donald W. C. Harris, October 8th, 2009.

144

SAME CHEMISTRY SET

Yes, we seem different, each person unique;
But it's our sameness, of which, I now speak!
No matter what language or shape of the cheek,
All have brave beauty beneath, where I seek!

Though we seem different in kinds of aspect,
Most of our **molecules** demand due respect!
Though each **human being** is **God**'s special project,
All are built with blocks from the **same chemistry set**!

All life has **purpose** with its destiny seal,
And it all plays a part in **humanity**'s wheel.
We learn from it too, when we **learn how to feel**;
The **essence of love** comes as **part of life's deal!**

Love all the **difference** you see on the cover;
Go under the surface to truly discover
The **sameness**, the **ONENESS**, the **power** to hover!
ONENESS makes **ALL**, the world's best lover!

Let all of us now become somewhat braver;
Touch the world by doing someone a favour!
Expect no return and do not waiver;
Somehow, somewhere, you are someone's life saver!

WE ALL CAME FROM
ONE AND THE SAME!

The above poem was written by Donald W. C. Harris 2010-08-02.
It expresses hope for peace and harmony throughout humanity.

SPIRIT DRIVEN MUSIC

Be right in with the music; get moving with its beat;
Hear its bright acoustics; set its rhythm in your feet!
Feel the drummer's drumsticks; listen to them speak!
Hypnotic is the message when the music's at its peak!

Language, does it matter? We all can understand
That music's universal, as it crosses every land!
Everyone can celebrate the soundings from a band,
That captures all vibrations found in every grain of sand!

Steady, like a heartbeat, the rhythm sets the pace;
Fascinating frequencies stir emotions in head space!
Better than any risky drugs, serotonin wins this race,
And happiness takes over, no matter where the place!

Energetic melodies sing out upon the beat;
Jubilation fills the air and no one takes a seat!
Dance and motion make the party; no one feels defeat!
No one wants to come unwound; no one hits delete!

Just keep this party going; it's fun for every one.
Keep dancing altogether, all night long into the sun.
Reverberations are all around; the whole world vibes as **ONE**!
There's love and joy for every soul; don't let us come undone!

Keep the spirit driven music, forever with us now;
Don't let our petty grievances intervene somehow.
Forgive and live; love, don't shove; forever we must plough
Soils for seeds to grow the fruits on **ONENESS'** abundance bough!

EVERY SOUL IN ONE BOWL
MAKE MUSIC, TOGETHER!

The above poem was written by Donald W. C. Harris 2010-08-27.

THE ONLY RACE...
FOR ALL TO WIN!

There's only one race and we all are in it;
From our moment of birth we're set to begin it.
Right from the start, we're determined to win it...
Our potential together is endlessly infinite.

No matter what challenge is placed in our way...
No matter ill feelings our neighbours display...
No matter the hurt that some folks may say,
The glory of this victory is for all one fine day.

We all must be winners to muster the prize!
To all get there first, we must stop spreading lies,
Respect others' values; place trust in the eyes;
See only their love, not things to despise!

Once we've done that and we've all crossed the line,
Life for all persons will be nothing but fine.
So, put on your runners; join this race so divine...
It's the one human race! Make it yours! Make it mine!

BLESS ALL! LOVE ALL!

Written for everyone, by Donald W. C. Harris, July 14th, 2007.

TOGETHER IN ONENESS

"Here I sit in my power chair;
Who's my next victim? I don't care!
I'll break them down and give a scare…
For I'm in control; there's no need to be fair!"

"Now here's a guy who's five minutes late.
I'll make him puke the food from his plate.
My harsh and brutal voice will grate
On his nerves. I'll make his flesh fish bait!"

Why must officials be so rude?
So many aren't nice, and often plain crude.
Whether a woman, or some guy dude,
Some take liberties that are even lewd!

Some poor soul on this telephone line,
Says, "Good morning…I hope everything's fine."
The boss yells back, "I'm *goona* break *yer* spine!"
And the well-wisher tries to listen…benign!

ONE knows you enjoy your power position;
Even that you like fresh blood from incision…
And you cut deeply; feel no inhibition.
Now, it's time for your brand new rendition!
Instead of dictating terms and conditions,
Why not try listening to your victims' positions?
Understand feelings of persons with missions!
Together, in **ONENESS**; don't set up partitions!

MAKE ALL THINGS WORK, TOGETHER!

The above poem was written by Donald W. C. Harris
May 22nd, 2009, for better relationships for everyone.

148

UNIVERSE CHI

I am you and you are me!
Combined, we two are more than three.
One is more than there ever needs be;
One is everyone! **One** is **All**! See?

I am in you and you are in me!
All are part of the **same gene pool tree**!
All are enveloped by **Universe chi**!
All are **empowered by Spirit** free!

Nothingness is **everything to All**, everyone;
Clearing all heads of stuff and of scum,
Makes room for the light of Spirit's bright sun:
The energy source for all systems to run!

If a head is crowded with thoughts of its own,
It puts too much weight on shoulders and bone!
Let this load go; **Spirit's seeds will get sown**;
Become enlightened with **new wisdom** shown!

Letting the **Power of Universe chi**,
Come into our lives and letting it be
The **guide for whole living** entirely,
Seems **principally sound** and **spiritually free**!

ONENESS IS KEY
TO A UNIVERSE FREE!

The above poem was written by Donald W. C. Harris
2008-09-22 (verses 1-4) and 2011-10-22 (verse 5).

UNIVERSE THAT'S PRETTY

ALL belong to **ONENESS' UNI-VERSE-CITY!**
It grants degrees in **tolerance of diversity**.
ALL of **ONENESS' students** have perspicacity,
And also demonstrate considerable elasticity…

So they can see **worthiness** in **ultra-simplicity**.
Caution! ONENESS does not condone any **acts of duplicity!**
Draw upon **wisdom, trust** wholly and implicitly
In **commingling discoveries** of **university** and **UNI-VERSE-CITY,**
In order to **discern good and right** from disgusting perversity!
ONENESS grows in popularity by overcoming adversity!

University mostly trains its students by emphasizing **subject content;**
UNI-VERSE-CITY dwells on **behavioural dynamics** of the moment,
And on **interactions**: forgive, love, share, fair, help, comfort, consent.
Be grateful for the stickiness of **Humanity's 'cement'**!

UNI-VERSE-CITY is **devoted** to the **only team that matters,**
Which, is **all** of **Humanity; all** of **GOD's children** are the **batters,**
In the **game** that does away with **evil force** that **shatters**
Our dreams; if we strike out, all our **hopes it scatters!**
We must change our world, before it's totally in tatters!

Every person must enter **ONENESS' UNI-VERSE-CITY,**
And **graduate with honours in tolerance of diversity!**
Accommodate differences! Make **humanity** united, strong and gritty!
What's our **ultimate reward**? A **universe that's pretty!**

ALL NEED UNIVERSITY…AND
UNI-VERSE-CITY! GET IT!

The above poem was written by Donald W. C. Harris March 10th, 2010.
(Use of the term 'uni-verse' comes from a
suggestion by Donald's spouse.)

WORLD NEEDS LEADERS...
MAYBE YOU?

This world needs leaders...maybe you?
To coach, harmoniously, in all we do;
To blend blacks, whites and shades of blue,
Browns and yellows and every hue.

What finer prize than just to know
Arts of love, respect, and how to grow.
Imagine: warm comfort when there is no foe!
Surely **ONENESS** is the way to go!

For no other route to peace and bliss,
Can offer more than the **ONENESS** kiss.
While other acts draw boos and hiss,
ONENESS blessings just can't miss!

So won't you join the **ONENESS** train?
To endless benefits, like sprouting grain...
Enough for **ALL** to shed aches and pain
From hunger? **ONENESS** efforts strike again!

Be my guest, now...Come aboard!
We'll discover how not to hoard.
Share **GOD**'s graces. We've so ignored
Opportunities for **ONENESS, LORD!**

ONENESS IS WHOLE HARMONY!

Written for hope of a wholesome world of happiness, By
Donald W. C. Harris, July 31st, August 1st, 2008.

WRITING POEMS IS MY SONG

Writing poems is **my song to sing**;
I do it better than anything.
It makes me whole, like a golden ring;
My gift from spirit makes me sing

Of **love**, **trust**, **kindness** and **sharing fun**,
And **all good things for helping ONE**
Spread wings wide for flight to sun,
Taking with it, **every one**!

I love to read my poetry,
Wherein are **messages meant for me**
(**And all others**, hopefully).
Universality is **ONENESS'** key.

Themes of **ONENESS' totality**
Come to me in my writing spree,
Flowing freely, naturally;
Right words well up, amazingly!

Poems are **my passion** now;
My purpose: teach clearly how
ONENESS bears a fruitful bough,
Yielding **PEACE** and **POWER**...**Wow**!

3 R'S: READING, WRITING & RIGHTING!

The above poem was written by Donald W. C.
Harris upon waking, March 9th, 2010.

YOU ARE ONE WITH ALL

Are **you** content with every thought?
Or feel like cold's nose, filled with snot?
Or hold emotions gnarled in knot?
Or blood, slow-flowing, about to clot?

Are **you** afraid to sign the dot...
That seals the deals for something bought?
The things **you** think that mean a lot...
Are only traps of **person**al plot.

In truth, **you**'ve not a thing to fear;
And only joy should cause a tear...
For **GOD** is good! That is so clear.
Knowing this...is comfort dear.

All thoughts and deeds are interactive...
None independent, but like a laxative,
Move through **UNIVERSE**...chain-reactive...
Gliding, sliding...unstopped by sieve!

Be aware of your significance here!
You're part of **everything**, far and near...
A diamond rough...with value dear!
You are **ONE** with **ALL**...that's clear!

And everything **you** say or do,
Improves or harms a part of **you**...
For **you** extend beyond the blue!
Your endless reach grips **ALL**...that's true!

YOU REACH THE UNIVERSE!
DO RIGHT THINGS RIGHT!

The above poem was written by Donald W.
C. Harris February 15th, 2009
for all to benefit in a better world of oneness.

153

PEACE

ALWAYS FORGIVE!

Forget what you may...but always forgive!
There-in's a code we all need to live.
Think not what to take...but more, how to give,
Then greed can pass through us as holes of a sieve.

Dwell not on worry; get doing your best,
To help the others face up to life's test,
To discover their purpose and rise to their crest.
On this path to glory, there's peace in the nest.

We all can discover our reason for being,
Our own precious peaks to better our seeing,
Let's grow our skills; become masters agreeing.
We all must contribute with none of us fleeing.

All of us have magic hearts of gold.
Step up to the plate! Let your kindness unfold!
I know it takes courage to be brave and bold,
But you'll find peace of mind and self glory untold.

For you'll know you were there for others in need;
You'll know that in them you'll have planted that seed
That helps them sprout forth and take up the lead
So they can contribute like you did, indeed!

BLESS ALL CHILDREN
AND SINGLE PARENTS!

Written August 14th, 2007, by Donald W. C. Harris, while thinking
of children who have lost a parent; may these children find quickly, their
courage of spirit needed to mature suddenly and often, unexpectedly.

EYES CLOSED...

Eyes closed...**I** see clearly now...
My mission...teach **others** how
To find work fun...sweat on brow!
Respect **all life**...a **tree**, a **cow**!

Every moment occurs one time;
Make each count much...none subprime!
Do just right things; commit no crime!
Help **another**; pay **your** dime!

Be a steward of **one** lost **soul**!
Teach how to fill an empty bowl,
And figure how to stay off dole!
Helping **others** is now their goal!

Across the world with **ONE** intent,
Every **person,** just goodness bent...
Not **one** would be without a tent!
All gifts from **GOD** are heaven sent!

ALL can share in **Earth**'s abundance;
Enjoy belonging; celebrate **ONE**'s dance!
Stand up tall! Maintain that stance!
ONENESS marks **our** grandest trance!

Nothing more need be written or said.
ALL world's **peoples** have now been fed.
ALL are now leaders who have been led
To worthy **ONENESS**...far from dead!

ONENESS...OUR MOST
WORTHY GOAL!

Written for **ALL** to be in peaceful harmony,
by Donald W. C. Harris, June 13th, 2009.

FOR ALL, WITHOUT FIGHT!

Going to war makes all people sore;
All who were friends may not be, any more!
Life drops away or gets stained by the gore.
There's never a winner, just rot to the core!

There isn't a gain by launching attacks.
Or sneaking advantage with stabs into backs.
It's futile to punch and abuse one with smacks!
Has war any logic? It's flawed fully with cracks!

Isn't it wiser to better perform
By showing kind feelings, tender and warm?
Know that we're brothers, none of us norm,
Here, **ALL** must sleep in **ONE**'s common dorm!

We need to know that **WE are ALL ONE**,
And no one's worth more, under Earth's sun;
We are all winners! Yes, we all have won
The right to belong with **GOD** and **THE SON**!

If all feel and know, and do what is right,
Then, starting now, we can all find **GOD**-light,
And never stray far from the path lit so bright,
That leads to **abundance**, for all, without fight!

ALL NEEDS CAN BE MET
WHEN ONENESS IS SET!

The above poem was written by Donald W. C. Harris 2010-11-07.
It was written for all life to flourish to full purpose in a peaceful world.

159

HEAR SILENCE!

Listen to the **silence** of the **sea**,
When it's **still** as it ever could be!
All **coalesced droplets** feel free,
United, in **peaceful harmony**!

Listen to the **light** of the **moon**;
It always **sings** its **beautiful tune**,
Of **light-filled love for the loon**,
And all things; graced we are by this boon!

Listen to the **silence** of the **wind**!
It can **calm** those chagrined,
And those overwhelmed and dinned,
By **noise from thinking they've sinned**!

Listen to the **quiet** of the **mind**!
When it's **open, troubles unwind**;
Peace returns when one is **kind**!
Let **spirit** in! Don't shut the blind!

Listen to the **silence** of the **stars**!
Exploding **vibes go to planets like Mars**,
As **rhythmic music** in **meaningful bars**,
Meant for **peace in the universe**, not wars!

PEACE FOR ALL IS
THE BEST CHOICE
& IS MEANT TO BE!

The above poem was written by Donald W. C. Harris 2010-03-19.

KEY TO PEACE

Find **your** calling...what **you**'re meant to do.
What's best for **ALL**? **Your** best "**YOU**" true.
Take quiet time; search the inner "**YOU**",
For what brings most satisfaction, too!

Look for something **others** need;
Then determine to take the lead...
Without being selfish, or showing greed!
Therein's **your** key to **peace**, indeed.

Should **you** supply a new invention,
Creative goods with kind intention,
Or some idea that improves convention...
Then **you**'re on track to **life** worth mention!

Or maybe **you**'ll give service better,
With dedication to the letter,
To give **your** all...a real go-getter!
Stay relaxed! Be not a fretter!

Be sure to maintain ethics fair,
And show **your clients, you** do care
That **they** are pleased...not stripped bare!
Your bizzes can flourish anywhere!

You'll feel good with contribution
To some aspect of **human** solution
Without distraction or dilution.
Help build **ONENESS**' constitution!

PEACE TO ALL!

Written for **ALL** to find **PEACE**,
by Donald W. C. Harris, October 4th, 2009.

MALICIOUS MILITIAS

Malicious militias seem downright vicious;
And often, **their members** appear quite officious.
Of evil militias, **we** should **all** be suspicious,
For events, often ugly, stem from over-ambitious...
Like craps in toilets, militias have niches.

Attacks on **our brothers** will not solve what matters!
The hatred...it grows...and **life** breaks and shatters.
War splits **us** apart...**our family**...it scatters.
What a mess to deal with! Ruins and **blood** splatters.
Our bodies and **souls**...**they** end up in tatters.

Fighting is so pointless; results even futile,
For it leaves only rubble...bits and pieces to pile.
War grates **us** harshly, like the rasp of a file,
And still, in the end, **we** must **all** reconcile.
Oh, when will **we** learn how to gain the last mile?

Nothing is gained...from exploding a bomb,
Or from sending a missile to disrupt the calm,
From wrecking fine works built from sweat in the palm.
What often helps more is a soother or psalm.
Peace is the prize! Wouldn't that be awesome?
Remember the mess left by war in Viet Nam!

PEACE BE TO ALL...FOR ONE EVERLASTING MOMENT!

Written for **our world family**, with **love** to **all persons** and **planets**,
by Donald W. C. Harris, mid-July, 2007
(verse four added July 11th, 2009).

MESSENGERS OF HOPE

Let's all be **messengers of hope,**
Whether Christian, Moslem or other scope.
None of us is meant to grope
In darkness on a slippery slope.

We've all let things get pretty bad;
Our present state is very sad.
It's time for every lass and lad
To restore and better what we had.

Each of us must do our part
To spread the love that's in our heart.
Think a little before we start...
Do what's right; that's what's smart.

And do it all anonymously,
Expecting no reward we see.
All the good we'll do's the key,
For **all** of **us** to be **me, we** and free.

Show respect and care for neighbours,
Consistently, without waivers.
Be trusting friends, not enslavers;
That way we'll all be life savers!

Yes, all we need are messengers of hope,
So none of us need ever mope...
Or ever feel the label **"dope"**.
Let's clean up! Get out the soap!

Written by Donald W. C. Harris, April 5th, 2008 in contribution
to the new movement to better our world soon.

NEW YEAR'S DAY

New Year's Day starts over again,
Another year…two thousand and ten;
Three hundred sixty-five more days…and then,
Another new year will start once again.

No doubt each day will hold much in store,
And a lot of **people** will surely keep score,
To see **who**, among **us**, may be taking more.
Such futile chores would be best to ignore!

Trying to account for **who** has **what**,
Often leads to **industries** closed **shut**;
Then, **unemployment** becomes a **glut**,
While **sickness** settles in the **nation's gut**!

Desperate people may do bad things,
And cling together in **gangs** and **rings**
That **punish innocence** with **evil stings**!
In absence of **PEACE, LIFE** barely clings!

With greed and violence prevalent,
Peaceful doves can make little dent…
Unless **each loves all** with **determined intent**,
Wars and **fighting** cannot relent!

NOW is the moment for **ALL** to endorse
A change of direction from present course.
GOODWILL, is the **WORKABLE FORCE**,
To emplace the **POWER** of **ONENESS SOURCE**!

EXTEND GOODWILL TO ALL!

Written for **ALL** to be welcomed into the **PEACE** of **ONENESS**,
by Donald W. C. Harris, November 28th, 2009.

ONE'S PURPOSE...PEACE

ONE's purpose is **PEACE**
For **ALL**...not to cease...
With fairness her grease,
ONE SPIRIT release!

Smooth **WORLD** with no edges,
No cliffs, no sharp wedges...
ALL have privileges...
ALL FREE beyond hedges!

ALL joined *"pseudo-nations"*
Override accusations;
Make compensations
To stop **ALL**'s ablations!

ALL's wholeness prevails...
No hammers, no nails...
Just breezes, no gales...
Fill **HUMANITY**'s sails!

Together in strength,
WE ALL grow full length...
Making **ONE**'s mark,
Igniting **WORLD**'s spark!

GROW FULL LENGTH... TOGETHER!

Written for **ONE's PEACE**, by Donald W. C.
Harris, Sunday, January 18th, 2009.

ONLY TRAINING

Now, I'm only training others to kill!
Somehow, that still goes against my will;
In the end it means more bodies go still!
Can someone please help me swallow that pill?

"Thou shalt not kill" still rings in my ear,
From when I was young, before I drank beer.
I believed long ago that message so clear.
What happened since then? I'm filled now with fear!

Why am I teaching how to take **lives**?
Who grants me permission? Am I queen of all hives?
Why am I here sharpening the knives
Of **children as soldiers** who'll dance deadly jives?

Whatever happened to **brotherly love**?
There mustn't be extinction of the **global Peace Dove**!
Let its flight **unite all souls** from above!
Spirits know all of the secrets of

The **power of love** to bring **all folks together**;
Love binds all in friendship; all are bound by one tether.
Nothing unwinds this twine, no kind of weather!
Lighten all hearts: let's all float like a feather!

All human beings stem from the **same source**;
Knowing just this fact puts us **all on one course**:
An **all-for-one** course is a **most potent force**!
I ask all persons, "Please, **ONENESS**, do endorse!

STOP DEADLY JIVES!
SAVE LOVED ONES' LIVES!

The above poem was written by Donald W. C. Harris 2010-12-05.

PEACE OF ONE'S MIND

Education is bad if not broad;
If not wide enough to hold **God**,
The Father of all on Earth's sod;
Only **love wins His approval** and nod.
Without **God's love**, life's a fraud.

Responsible teachers educate;
Education goes way beyond indoctrinate,
And should never include how to hate;
Tolerance gives all a chance to elevate.
All are One so show patience! Negotiate!

Respect all sisters and bros,
And all in-betweens, for **God knows**
Each person reaps what one sows!
Love can make **friends** out of foes,
Make the effort! See how **friendship grows**!

Peace on Earth and out there in space,
Depends on **kindness** and **God's good grace**;
Do your part! Put a **smile on each face**!
Be a credit to **God's human race**!
Do your utmost! Succeed! Don't disgrace!

Let's all **restore faith in mankind**!
The **rewards** will shine silver-lined.
We'll **progress enlightened**, not blind,
Be enriched by treasures we'll find,
Especially the **PEACE of ONE'S MIND**!

TEACH WIDE APPRECIATION
FOR ALL OF GOD'S CREATION!

The above poem was written by Donald W. C. Harris 2012-09-18.

167

WALK WITH ONENESS

Take a **walk** with **ONENESS**...a **nature walk** is fine;
Its **sights** and **sounds** profound, ensure **you** stay the line.
Vibrations of the **PEACE** that's there, uplift **you** from decline,
And rejuvenate **SOUL**'s purpose, without the salt and brine!

The **beauty** of all **nature**, unspoiled by **human thought**,
Is simply how each setting, seems so suited to its spot,
Embracing all right elements, entwined without onslaught.
Total **PEACE** of **ONENESS** waits for **ALL** in **ONENESS** grot!

Each **walk** with **ONENESS** is a trip **you**'ll not forget...
A journey to a **perfect world**, along a **path** so set
To expose **you** to wondrous showers, yet never get **you** wet,
Along a **course** of **MIRACLES**! How much better can it get?

ALL PERSONS everywhere, need to find the **ONENESS** route!
All egos, in the end, must be infinitely dilute:
No other **path** is eligible, for no one can refute
ONENESS works! Its **way** gives **ALL** a truly winning suit!

Know that **ALL** are **ONE**...and that's a **good** thing too;
That **all your deeds** done to **OTHERS**, happen back to **YOU**.
Stop! Before **YOU** act unfairly to **OUR** extended zoo,
Know **ONENESS** guides **HUMANITY**
on righteous trails! That's true!

WALK FOR ONENESS!

Written for **ALL** to find **PEACE** in their walk with **ONENESS**,
by Donald W. C. Harris, March 1st, 2009.

TIME

FOCUS ON NOW'S VIBRATION!

When **you** drive...keep **mind** on the drive.
If it's not...your body may not survive!
Others' bodies too, may not stay alive;
Lives may pass...only **SPIRITS** will thrive!

If **one**'s attention falls one bit short,
One might as well be engaged in sport;
Or be tripped out by a cocaine snort!
One accident...case may go to court!

What if one dies? **GOD**, that's so sad!
Think how that affects mom and dad.
Loss might kill **them** too...that's bad!
Don't let that happen...**all** will be glad!

Should **one** live...but injured be,
One's **life** could change dramatically,
Depending on just how seriously
One's been hurt; now **all** should see

That driving safely is **one**'s obligation;
A responsibility of **global nation**;
One's duty to **life**'s preservation!
Keep focus on **NOW'S VIBRATION!**

BE HERE NOW...IN THE GIFT OF THE PRESENT!

Written for **all life** everywhere, by Donald W. C. Harris, June 5th, 2009.
(Note: Inspiration to write this poem stemmed from a
Dr. Phil T.V. show, seen June 1st, 2009.)

HISTORICAL FACT THAT ALL SHOULD KNOW

It was **four score and ten years ago**,
In downtown Calgary, by the river Bow,
Calgary First Spiritualist Church began to grow!
That's historical fact that all should know!

It was Sunday school for kids at the very start,
A lyceum, which became an essential part
Of the **British Spiritualist Union**'s throbbing heart!
C.F.S.C. was chartered in Alberta in 1920 to impart

Spiritual teachings of Andrew Jackson Davis to
Just a few kids in attendance, and later adults, too.
Attendance was sporadic; the church struggled for a few,
Until the Harshman sisters and their mom came into view!

Rev. Harry Collett dedicated this Hillhurst site in 1974.
Rev. David Oliver and Avril served here, thirty years and more!
C.F.S.C. now thrives with members, courses and workshops galore!
Seven Principles still guide the way and will forevermore!

Meaningful meditations and mediumships take place;
Healing and miracle matters and more topics we embrace;
Some come here for comfort from their so-called falls from grace.
Is it not true that **God** has no intent to disgrace?
We're truly grateful for this warm and wonderful worship space!

NEVER BE LEFT IN A LURCH! JOIN CALGARY FIRST SPIRITUALIST CHURCH!

The above poem was written by Donald W. C.
Harris 2010-09-29 at request of C.F.S.C.

IT'S ALWAYS TODAY

After today begins a brand new today;
I wouldn't want it any other way!
Tomorrow has no chance to stay;
Yesterdays are gone! That's okay!

Present time is meaningful to my being!
Only the moment is all I'm seeing!
Savour the moment ever fleeing!
Dealing with now sets one's freeing!

Each moment lasts for so little time;
If not in it fully, it's not worth a dime!
Time slips away; that's a subtle crime.
Moments gone are hills one can't re-climb!

All feel short of time to do what needs be done;
Living in the moment assures results more fun!
Loving every moment welcomes warmth of sun,
That comforts one along the path that's best for everyone!

Look upon today with utmost positive thought;
Know that all you tackle falls into proper slot.
Good things will come to you, and bad will simply rot.
When every person does the same, that's when we'll all be caught

In present time together, in tune with **ONENESS'** plot,
That's open to **all souls** to be put in just one pot;
Stirred and mixed together, it's the best stew that we've got!
It's one that holds forever, every moment's treasured spot!

NOW IS HOW!

The above poem was written by Donald W. C. Harris 2010-10-25.

MY SEVEN SCORE

I'm seventy-three, no longer, no more…
Because after today, I'll be seventy-four!
I'll be well on my way to my seven score;
And after that, who could want any more?

I'm writing this now, at the end of December;
If I don't finish, I won't need to remember!
At any time, my bones could dismember;
I may be cremated and reduced to an ember!

I'm carrying on from one year to the next…
It's quite a chore once the brain gets perplexed!
Seeing through lenses, both thick and convex,
It's asking a lot, just to read some fine text!

Time has no meaning for those over the hill;
Nothing's important when just staying still.
Even just breathing, may counter one's will…
Once in this state, has one had one's fill?

Unless you find something of interest to you,
You might just as well be stuck in a zoo…
A curious creature for people to view,
Until you drop dead! Even that, may be taboo!

But I'll always know that my soul carries on,
Maintained by good spirits, each passing dawn;
While I've been around, I've never been gone…
And I've given my best to **HUMANITY**'s bond!

ONLY 66 YEARS MORE…
WILL MAKE MY SEVEN SCORE!

Dec. 28, 2009 Donald W.C. Harris wrote this poem
in anticipation of his seventy fourth birthday.

PRESENT TIME...THE GIFT OF NOW

The **present**...It's everyone's **gift**; **Live** it **now**!
The **past**...It's already buried by plough;
The **future**...It's not yet fruit on the bough;
So get with the **now**! You've got to, somehow!

People who linger in grievances gone,
Can never experience a brand new dawn;
They've ceased all growth; their branches are sawn.
They might as well have the brains of morons.

For those who look forward and plan ahead,
But fail to act as each moment is shed,
Lose out on living each blessing they're fed;
Yes, these are lost souls of the already dead.

For **meaningful moments**, it comes down to this;
Give **love** when you can! Relish **hugs** and a **kiss**!
Care for all people as true brother and sis,
And never be cruel! Offer **kindness**, not hiss!

You can be more when **living** the **present**.
While tending the needs of others, be **pleasant**!
Enjoy **Mother Nature**...her trees, or a pheasant,
The **light** of the moon, whether full, or just crescent!

Start living now! Break away from restraints!
Smell **flower**'s **fragrance**! Don't dwell on complaints!
Embrace natural flow; enjoy what it paints!
Won't you **become now, one** of **ONENESS**' great saints?

ACCEPT YOUR GIFT! LIVE NOW!

Written by Donald W. C. Harris, November 22nd, 2009,
for those who feel held back from the joys of life.

SPRING FEVER IS SPREADING

Spring jumpstarts new **hope** every year!
Hikers and cyclists get out their gear;
Crocuses too, make it all so clear…
The time for gardening is very near!

Groundhogs have all had their say;
Even "Jack Frost" has gone away!
Spring fever is spreading! That's quite okay
With all of us 'kids', who, love to play

In the sunshine and warmth of each new day.
Tho spring starts in March, soon will come May;
A few April showers will not likely stay,
But will welcome the flowers, along the way.

All is beautiful, with green shoots and grass,
In meadows in mountains, through every pass,
Laden with wetlands and **life** forms en masse.
Preserve natural beauty! Don't be an ass!

Sustaining the birds, the bees and the trees,
Means that we cannot just do as we please;
Don't let spring fever become a disease!
Love ALL as **ONE**! **Now,** on bended knees!

SPRING EVOKES HOPE.

The above poem was written by Donald W. C. Harris March '06, 2010.

Printed in the United States
By Bookmasters